Antiracist Pedagogy in Action

Antiracist Pedagogy in Action

Curriculum Development from the Field

Edited by Erin T. Miller and Angela V. Walker

ROWMAN & LITTLEFIELD
Lanham • Boulder • New York • London

Published by Rowman & Littlefield
An imprint of The Rowman & Littlefield Publishing Group, Inc.
4501 Forbes Boulevard, Suite 200, Lanham, Maryland 20706
www.rowman.com

86-90 Paul Street, London EC2A 4NE

Copyright © 2023 by Erin T. Miller and Angela V. Walker

All rights reserved. No part of this book may be reproduced in any form or by any electronic or mechanical means, including information storage and retrieval systems, without written permission from the publisher, except by a reviewer who may quote passages in a review.

British Library Cataloguing in Publication Information Available

Library of Congress Cataloging-in-Publication Data

Names: Miller, Erin T., editor. | Walker, Angela V., editor.
Title: Antiracist pedagogy in action : curriculum development from the field / Edited by Erin T. Miller and Angela V. Walker.
Description: Lanham : Rowman & Littlefield Publishers, [2023] | Includes bibliographical references. | Summary: "This book provides precise definitions and concrete examples to demonstrate how antiracist pedagogy is a way of teaching and learning that engages past failures of American democracy in order to inspire students to take action toward fulfilling the promise of American democracy"—Provided by publisher.
Identifiers: LCCN 2022042061 (print) | LCCN 2022042062 (ebook) | ISBN 9781475867862 (cloth) | ISBN 9781475867879 (paperback) | ISBN 9781475867886 (ebook)
Subjects: LCSH: Racism in education—United States. | Multicultural education—United States. | Anti-racism—Study and teaching—United States. | Racism—Study and teaching—United States. | Curriculum planning—United States. | Culturally relevant pedagogy—United States.
Classification: LCC LC212.2 .A65 2023 (print) | LCC LC212.2 (ebook) | DDC 370.117—dc23/eng/20221019
LC record available at https://lccn.loc.gov/2022042061
LC ebook record available at https://lccn.loc.gov/2022042062

Contents

	Editors' Acknowledgments	vii
	Foreword *Dr. Adell Cothorne,* *Loyola University of Maryland, School of Education*	ix
Introduction	The Role of Antiracist Pedagogy in Democratic Education *Angela V. Walker, Erin T. Miller,* *and Scott R. Gartlan*	1
Chapter 1	Antiracist Pedagogy: An Overview *Erin T. Miller and Angela V. Walker*	7
Chapter 2	Dismantling Internalized Anti-Black Racism in Literature Instruction through Racial Identity Reflection *Angela V. Walker*	17
Chapter 3	Justice Is More Important Than Kindness: Antiracist Pedagogy in a First-Grade Classroom *Anne Galligan*	29
Chapter 4	Middle School English Language Arts: My Personal Story of Exploration, Empowerment, and Antiracist Teaching *Seun Omitoogun*	39

Chapter 5	Confronting Scientific Racism and Eugenics in a Freshman Biology Course *Pablo Chialvo*	51
Chapter 6	A Revised Narrative of the Civil Rights Movement and the Power of People in a High School History Course *Elizabeth Veilleux Haynes*	65
Chapter 7	Middle School Science Students Learn How Structural Racism in the US Shaped Our COVID Experience *Evie Elson*	81
	Necessary Damage: A Conclusion *Angela V. Walker and Erin T. Miller*	95
	About the Authors	97

Editors' Acknowledgments

One is only a teacher because one was taught to be. I have had many teachers in my life. Some of them are featured in this book. Some know me; others do not. Malik Norman, Zetta Elliott, and Sam Tanner are teachers I know whose lives happened to intersect with mine during the time that the ideas for this book were forming. They touched every word of these pages with their exquisite, honest pedagogy. Other teachers like Gholdy Muhammed and Bettina Love do not know they taught me, but I clung to their words during their many podcasts of 2020 to think more critically about my practice and who I wanted to be for my students. They also touched every word of these pages with their exquisite, honest pedagogy.

But it is my mother who taught me the most. She was a high school English teacher using antiracist pedagogies before there was a buzzword for them. Before they were lauded, feared, or hated. She just simply knew—she knew Black students in Orangeburg County, South Carolina, needed Black authors and pedagogies that centered their lives and histories. She was not trying to be a cool teacher. In fact, if questioned why she taught the way she did, she probably would have said something like, "Don't be ridiculous, that is just common sense." (She did not put up with things that were not commonsensical.) She knew her students needed more than the standard curriculum and so she just did her best. She did not claim or even try to be perfect and I loved that about her. She did not have the community I had in 2020 to develop or refine her pedagogies. So, she mostly did her work alone when she did not realize I was watching her, learning from her.

My mother will not read the pages of this book. But she touched every one of them with her exquisite, honest pedagogy. She is a part of me. And any part of me I share with you means a part of her is also shared. Her light and her intellect and her passion are not withering because I have made the promise to keep them burning bright. As long as I learn and teach and write, Dr. Susan S. Till will live with vitality and wisdom through me.

—Erin T. Miller

* * *

When referring to student behavior that interrupts the regular flow of activities in the classroom, teachers will often use the term disruptive. But the process of writing this book has helped me to understand that impactful teaching is also disruptive, intentionally so. I am immensely grateful for the teachers who disrupted my insecurity and self-doubt as a student. They agitated my comfort with only completing the assigned work and ignited a passion for pursuing the interests that were not stated in the assigned texts. From them, I learned to read between the lines and to write in the margins the conversations and ideas that were deliberately excluded. My contribution to this book is largely the result of their encouragement, which has extended well beyond the year that I sat in their classrooms.

To my students at all levels—high school, undergraduate, and graduate studies—I cannot remember a day when teaching them was not also a day of learning from them. Each day that I step into the classroom, I eagerly anticipate what they will say in response to the lessons I plan, the questions I ask, and the assumptions with which we wrestle every class period. They keep me on my toes, ever-evolving, always reflecting, and adjusting in my understanding of what it means to live as a citizen of this world.

And finally, to my mother who has always stressed the importance of an education and to my sister who has also taken up the charge to educate, it is wonderful to see this common thread in our legacy. May we continue to remain strong and committed to championing the power of an inclusive education and make ways for teaching where there are none.

—Angela V. Walker

Foreword

Dr. Adell Cothorne,
Loyola University of Maryland, School of Education

In American history, persons who identify as White have overwhelmingly been positioned as dominant while everyone else have been positioned as "other". Our founding fathers believed in freedom, justice, and the pursuit of happiness for all humans—as long as they were White. This is evidenced in the fact that most of the founding fathers themselves owned slaves. Thomas Jefferson was one of those founding fathers and continues to be lauded for how he sacrificed and fought for those coming to America in order to escape the tyranny of British rule. Yet, this same founding father felt impassioned and justified to put in writing the shortcomings of Blacks. In *Notes on the State of Virginia (1873),* Jefferson puts pen to paper to share with the world his thoughts on the limited intellectual ability and foul smell of Blacks. All this while he was repeatedly raping Sally Hemmings (a young slave girl) who was 14 years old, whereas Jefferson was 42. Jefferson and Hemmings created four living children while involved in this predatory on-going encounter. The quicker many White Americans can omit, erase, and obliterate the history, culture, and contributions of anyone who is not a straight, able-bodied, White male, the more comfortable this particular segment of the American population becomes. Your heroes are our monsters.

The authors believe antiracist pedagogy has a place in democratic education. However, inclusive education practices such as culturally relevant pedagogy and culturally responsive teaching do not hold precedent or importance in ethnostates. Many in the United States wish to push us to a time where citizenship is only extended to those who are classified as White.

Statistical demographics tell a story of a nation that is more diverse than it has ever been. There is a deceptive numbers game currently at play in the United States—a race of people that was once considered the "majority" are seeing their numbers decline in comparison to other racial groups. It is not surprising that a few powerful (yet anonymous) people are trying to tilt the numbers. In 2021, the U.S. Census Bureau Population Estimates Program established that *White is any person having origins in any of the original peoples of Europe, the Middle East, or North Africa. It includes people who indicate their race as "White" or report entries such as Irish, German, Italian, Lebanese, Arab, Moroccan, or Caucasian.* It takes a quick Google search to determine that United States citizens descended from Arabian, Moroccan, or Lebanese ancestry are not what we typically classify as White in the United States. And while several people understand race is a social construct, to normalize social construction of knowledge is to acknowledge the process through which racial meaning is inherited, interpreted, and passed on from one generation to the next.

One may ask—Why is the *Antiracist Pedagogy in Action* text needed at this moment? The answer is simultaneously simple and multi-layered. Whether it was the Bray Schools for Enslaved Children in Colonial Virginia whose attendees faced persecution or death simply because they had learned the fundamentals of education or Pueblo children who were forced to leave their homes and attend boarding schools where they faced forced assimilation and genocide, American public education has always had a dark side when it comes to educating children deemed "other". The editors and authors of *Antiracist Pedagogy in Action* are doing double duty—exposing the educational sins of our past and providing antiracist pedagogy practices that can be used in school communities today to uplift, empower, and fortify ALL students.

As someone who has been an educator for over two (2) decades and has had the unique pleasure of educating scholars from the pre-kindergarten to the doctoral defense level, I know how impactful this book will be across the education spectrum. Academia can use it with pre-service teachers and future school leaders to analyze the type of instruction taking place and how to elevate that instruction. Educators can use *Antiracist Pedagogy in Action* to garner the success of each and every student. School district leaders and school boards can use the text to gain a deeper understanding of how their policies and practices impact the day-to-day operations of local schools and the next steps to take to improve the schooling experience for each student and his/her family.

Educators who engage in antiracist pedagogy are often very passionate about the work. That passion can translate into long days and nights, tired eyes, and an overwhelming sense of going 80,000 miles at a snail's pace. This work is necessary and exhausting. I am often asked—Dr. Cothorne, how do you stay whole as you continue to do this work. The answer for me is quite simple:

I AM SOMEBODY'S ANCESTOR!

Introduction

The Role of Antiracist Pedagogy in Democratic Education

Angela V. Walker, Erin T. Miller, and Scott R. Gartlan

> Precision in our language is important.
>
> —Clint Smith

This book is written by a diverse group of educators: three college instructors, five K–12 teachers, and the director of a professional development program for teachers. We spent the better part of one year learning about and implementing antiracist pedagogy. For most of us (Scott, Angela, Erin, Evie, Annie, and Elizabeth), our work together began through a unique inquiry-based professional development called the Charlotte Teachers Institute (CTI). CTI is a collaboration between university faculty at the University of North Carolina at Charlotte, Johnson C. Smith University, and local teachers in Mecklenburg County, North Carolina. CTI matches professors and teachers with similar interests in a small group seminar to learn about a wide variety of topics. The goal of CTI is to support K–12 teachers in creating curricular units about their topics that they can implement in K–12 classrooms and share with others. In our CTI seminar led by Erin, an associate professor at UNCC, we sat in the liminal space of antiracist theory and practice to respond to the question, "What does it mean to be an antiracist teacher?"

CTI's professional development model is aligned with features of effective teacher professional development. In a comprehensive review of thirty-five methodologically rigorous studies, Darling-Hammond, Hyler, and Gardner (2017) found seven features common to effective teacher professional development influencing student academic outcomes. CTI's model focuses on four that are particularly relevant here. First, effective professional development must focus on content. This particular CTI seminar focused on the content of antiracist theory and practice, and related content subject areas that teachers could fit within and across various grade levels. Second, high-quality professional development often creates a space for teachers to collaborate in meaningful ways. CTI organizes seminars through a diversity-focused lens creating groups with different grade levels, subject areas, and educational backgrounds. This composition of teachers in a seminar, coupled with content-focus and feedback and reflection time (point 3), contribute to a dynamic learning environment among teachers. Third, it is essential for professional development to be effective for it to build in time for teachers to reflect on the content and pedagogies discussed, situate that new learning within existing frameworks (or build new ones), and consider ways to integrate that new knowledge with engaging teaching practices. These seminars include scheduled one-on-one meeting times at two different points with each teacher and professor to discuss how the teacher sees themselves in the learning experience as they develop their written curriculum, various writing workshops that facilitate reflection and interactive discussion that leads to constructive feedback, and written feedback on the curriculum work to the teacher from the professor through a minimum of three revision-and-resubmission cycles. Fourth, research shows that effective professional development is provided over a sustained duration. CTI's professional development seminars take place over the course of seven months with teachers learning from and with the professor, as well as learning from each other over weekly, long-term, in-person, and virtual seminar meetings. In addition, four months of preparation time is provided for professors and lead teachers to discuss, reflect, and plan a specific learning experience for that group of teachers. This element of time enables other elements of effective professional development (e.g., content-focus, collaboration, feedback, and reflection) to develop and interact with the participating teachers and professor. It is this interactive component that situates each teacher at the center of the meaning-making process in CTI professional development seminars, a fundamental first step in transforming teacher knowledge, teaching practices, and ultimately student learning outcomes.

 For other contributors of this book (Seun and Pablo), our collaboration began when Angela and Erin, also college instructors teaching courses in a graduate certificate program in antiracism at UNCC, realized that some of their students (Seun and Pablo) were up to work similar to the CTI teachers in their own classroom spaces. The rest of the story is rather simple. Erin invited the teachers who had participated in CTI, and Angela and Erin invited students in their courses who were doing antiracist work in their educational spaces, to be a part of this book project. Seven educators agreed. The purpose of coming together to write this book is to clarify the phrase *antiracist pedagogy*. We also want to be explicit and transparent about the intentions we have when teaching students concepts about *race*, *racism*, and *antiracism*. Clint Smith (2021) reminds us that precision in our language is important when discussing race and racism. Without precision, grounds become fertile for misinterpretation and misrepresentation.

We hope our work is inspiring to other educators who want to learn more about antiracist pedagogy; more than that, we hope it provides a tool to engage with and speak back against repressive policies that seek to push out antiracist pedagogies. We worry that antiracist pedagogy has become a buzzword in scholarship and public discourse—simultaneously feared, silenced, hated, misunderstood, misused, and appropriated. It is both a popular trend among those seeking to be allies in response to recent civil unrest and a target of opposition among those who believe antiracism's theoretical underpinnings are anti-American. Roughly six months before our work in CTI began, a presidential memo from Donald Trump was released condemning antiracist pedagogy as "un-American" and "propaganda" (Voight, 2020). Yet, scholars who study antiracist pedagogy, such as Audrey Thompson (1997), describe it as *fundamentally* democratic. Our work took place within this contradictory and volatile public debate.

It is important to remember that although antiracist pedagogy entered and circulated in academic and pedagogical discourse three decades ago, teachers and scholars of Color have utilized the foundational ideas of antiracist pedagogy for centuries. Those educators knew the power of incorporating truthful histories of racism, as well as intentional education strategies to foster young people's resistance to racism. For example, many Black teachers have been influenced by writers and social critics like W. E. B. Dubois, Carter G. Woodson, Zora Neale Hurston, Angela Davis, and James Baldwin (Givens, 2021) who condemned the ways racism is reified in many school spaces. As a counternarrative, Afrocentric pedagogies were crafted around Black excellence in predominantly Black schools, summer schools called Freedom Schools (Hale, 2016; Jackson & Boutte, 2009) and literary societies (Muhammed, 2020). The power of youth activism to counteract racism was respected and cultivated by leaders like Ella Baker. Curricular overhauls took place in predominately white universities when students and leaders like Third World Liberation Front spokesperson Roger Alvarado organized and rallied against "white esteem curriculum" (Asante, 1991). Such activism spread across the nation and created many of the ethnic studies departments that thrive today in colleges and public schools. Students like Earnest Knocks Off, a Sicangu Lakota, starved himself to resist assimilation to whiteness in the Carlisle Indian Industrial School; while this was tragic reminder of the ways racist projects were carried out in school sites, it also a powerful reminder of how those same projects can be resisted. In other words, antiracist pedagogy as a term may be relatively new; it may be feared, hated, or embraced as essential. But, learning about racist histories and countering those through pedagogical action is as old as racism itself.

To be clear, we believe antiracist pedagogy has a place in democratic education. Therefore, we consider this book to be a clarifying project. In it, we provide precise definitions and concrete examples to demonstrate how antiracist pedagogy is a way of teaching and learning that engages past failures of American democracy in order to inspire students to take action toward fulfilling the promise of American democracy. We want to protect spaces for antiracist pedagogy because we, like Thompson (1997), are convinced that it is vital for the democratic health of our nation. Yet, we know that to do so means antiracist pedagogues like ourselves have work to do to better articulate and describe what we mean by antiracist pedagogy in action.

* * *

We begin this book in chapter 1 much like we began our work in CTI—searching for sharper distillations of theories of antiracist pedagogy to guide our practice. We launched our query in 2020 by reading literature, watching videos, listening to podcasts, and sharing our ideas for how we planned to take our theoretical learnings to practice during weekly Zoom meetings. We discussed what challenged us, what worried us, and what motivated us about what we learned. At the helm of every discussion were the students who would receive, reconstruct, and extend our pedagogical attempts to translate theory into curricular units. Using theory and practice, we contoured our collective understanding of antiracist pedagogy around particular defining characteristics. In chapter 1, Erin and Angela describe those, both drawing on existing literature as well as adding to it. Chapters 2 through 7 are stories from CTI participants and other invited teachers about how they enacted antiracist pedagogies in their classrooms. Each chapter is a contribution by an individual CTI participant or a student in the Antiracism Graduate Certificate Program: Angela Walker, Annie Galligan, Pablo Chialvo, Evie Elson, Elizabeth Hayes, and Seun Omitoogon. The chapters are developed around the characteristics of antiracist pedagogy we learned from Kishimoto (2018) and that we added from our own study. These stories are not intended to be scripts or templates. They were developed and implemented during a particular time shaped by a global pandemic, a national racial justice project, and a state-led tightening of the chokehold on conversations about race, racism, and antiracism. The chapters were developed and implemented with particular students in mind, spanning first-grade through college, across a variety of subject areas. It should also be clear that the authors do not situate themselves as experts. In fact, we reject the notion of individual expertise because it is a product of white supremacy culture (Okun, 2021) that works to move us as way from shared constructions of knowledge. What we offer here is an attempt to take what was learned about antiracist pedagogy in community with one another—leveraging the experience and courage of teachers committed to curricular activism to offer precise theoretical interpretations of what antiracist pedagogy looked like across diverse curricular spaces during the 2020–2021 and 2021–2022 academic years.

References

Asante, M. K. (1991). Afrocentric curriculum. *Educational leadership*, 49(4), 28–31.
Darling-Hammond, L., Hyler, M. E., & Gardner, M. (2017). *Effective teacher professional development*. Palo Alto, CA: Learning Policy Institute.
Givens, J. R. (2021). *Fugitive pedagogy: Carter G. Woodson and the art of Black teaching*. Harvard University Press.
Hale, J. N. (2016). *The freedom schools: Student activists in the Mississippi civil rights movement*. Columbia University Press.
Jackson, T. O., & Boutte, G. S. (2009). Liberation literature: Positive cultural messages in children's and young adult literature at freedom schools. *Language Arts*, 87(2), 108–116.
Kishimoto, K. (2018). Anti-racist pedagogy: From faculty's self-reflection to organizing within and beyond the classroom. *Race Ethnicity and Education*, 21(4), 540–554.
Muhammad, G. (2020). *Cultivating genius: An equity framework for culturally and historically responsive literacy*. Scholastic Incorporated.
Okun, T., & James, K. (2000). White supremacy culture. *Dismantling racism: A workbook for social change groups*. Change Work. https://www.dismantlingracism.org/white-supremacy-culture.html.
Smith, C. (2021). *How the word is passed: A reckoning with the history of slavery across America*. Little, Brown and Company.
Thompson, A. (1997). For: Anti-racist education. *Curriculum Inquiry*, 27(1), 7–44. https://doi.org/10.1111/0362-6784.00035.
Vought, R. (2020). Memorandum for the heads of executive departments and agencies. (Report No. M-20-34). https://www.whitehouse.gov/wp-content/uploads/2020/09/M-20-34.pdf.

CHAPTER ONE

Antiracist Pedagogy

An Overview

Erin T. Miller and Angela V. Walker

The conceptual underpinnings of the term antiracist pedagogy were born out of the failure of multicultural education and other liberal reforms of the mid–twentieth century to critically address racism in America through pedagogical projects. Because of the overt focus on structural racism and power as the epicenter of antiracist pedagogy, it is conceptualized as both potentially overlapping with and operating as a point of departure from other ideological and philosophical embodiments of pedagogy that attune to race and culture (Kailin, 2002). For example, the traditions of culturally sustaining pedagogy (Paris & Alim, 2014), culturally relevant pedagogy (Ladson-Billings, 1995), and culturally responsive teaching (Gay, 2010) are built upon more than a century of Black, Latinx, and Indigenous "thought pioneers" (Nash et al., 2020, p. 7) and create spaces for critical praxis in education (Baines et al., 2018). Yet, it is possible to engage with these orientations and not overtly centralize the dismantling of structural racism.

In contrast, antiracist pedagogy—drawing on critical theory and interpretive theory—specifically deploys teaching strategies that encourage students to consider the role of racialized power, privilege, and oppression. This is accomplished both in terms of analyzing society, as well as critically reflecting on one's own position within it. Blakeney (2005) defined antiracist pedagogy as a paradigm located within critical theory used "to explain and counteract the persistence and impact of racism," using both knowledge and action to "promote social justice for the creation of a democratic society in every respect" (p. 119). Antiracist pedagogy aims to transform racist structures by challenging individuals and systems that perpetuate racism (Kailin, 2002). Within antiracist pedagogy, the process of teaching and learning is as critically important as the content being taught (Wagner, 2005). It is important to remember that antiracist pedagogy is not focused on reaching uniform or "ready-made outcomes" (Kishimoto, 2018, p. 542); rather, it is fundamentally emergent, or focused on learning as an evolving, effective strategy for social movements that work for racial and economic justice. Undergirded by antiracist theory, antiracist pedagogy attends to power in order to actively resist racism (Thompson, 1997; Zamalin, 2019). To accomplish this, notions of race neutrality or racial innocence are rejected (Blakeney, 2005). In other words, like antiracism more generally, antiracist pedagogy assumes that racism is alive and well and strives to counteract it.

While these theoretical descriptions of antiracist pedagogy are helpful, Kishimoto (2018) extended and clarified these assertions by specifying that that antiracist pedagogy involves three central characteristics: (1) infusing content related to race and racism into teaching, (2) utilizing particular pedagogical approaches, and (3) antiracist organizing/activism. In what follows, we describe how we conceptualized these characteristics to design antiracist pedagogical units in first grade through college education spaces.

The Infusion of Content Related to Race and Racism

While it may seem obvious that in order to enact antiracist pedagogy, teachers would need to possess content related knowledge about race and racism, many Americans in general do not have a detailed or accurate understanding of our county's historical lineage of racial oppression (Fleming, 2006). Considering the ways that slavery in particular is taught, the author and social critic Clint Smith argued, "We don't have a shared collective understanding of how we arrived at this moment, and we don't share a collective grounding in the history that created the conditions of our contemporary landscape" (Dennis, 2021, para. 4). Despite the problems with not having a collective grounding as it relates to our country's relationship to oppressive practices, Smith's words should not surprise us. Most of us were schooled in dominant narratives that whitewashed and sanitized stories of racism and antiracism during our K–12 experiences (Du Bois, 1973; Wynter, 2003). To date, these are not widely corrected in teacher education programs (King & Swartz, 2015). This is true despite the fact that the hallmarks of popular pedagogical theories taught in teacher education, particularly in relation to the education of youth of Color, suggest the importance of knowing your students and leveraging their cultural assets and histories (Dillard, 2021; Ladson-Billings,

1999; Gay, 2010). Despite this, teacher education programs do not do an adequate job teaching the histories, resistances, legacies, and excellence of minoritized people (Love, 2019; Muhammed, 2020; for a notable exception, see Wynter-Hoyte & Smith, 2020).

It is important to shed light on this gap because historical knowledge of race, racism, and antiracism is an essential component of antiracist pedagogy. Pedagogical attempts to integrate issues related to race, racism, and antiracism are best taken up within their historical, social, and political contexts. Yet, if this content is not known by teachers because they themselves have not been taught or have not taken it upon themselves to learn, teachers walk on precarious slopes in their attempts to integrate learning about race, racism, and antiracism in their pedagogies. Incorporating discussions with students about racism—for example, pushout discipline policies (Morris, 2016), racist policing (Smith, 2021), "white-esteem curriculum" (Asante, 1991), tone policing (Saad, 2020)—in isolation from the historical, social, and political worlds from which they arise is superficial and ill-conceived.

It is also imperative to contextualize antiracist pedagogy within historical, cultural, and political contexts because, in the absence of such positionings, antiracist pedagogy could be reduced to moral educational reform movement rather than a rigorous analysis of race relations. Moral education reform movements are concerned with shaping individual behavior according to a prescribed notion of good or bad. Learning about racism in isolation from its historical, social, and political milieu is likely to reinforce binary notions of good/non-racist people and actions from bad/racist people and actions. Not only does this one-dimensional framing negate the complexity and intersectionality of identity, it does nothing to engage in collective resistance to and transformation of unjust racial dynamics. Yet, resistance to and transformation of racial injustice are centralizing elements of antiracist pedagogy.

Centering Joy and Historical Resistance to Racism

Learning about the racial oppression of minoritized groups must go hand in hand with learning about how those same groups actively resisted oppression. This is important because challenging racist structures is a part of antiracist pedagogy. To best challenge racism, it is helpful to understand how racism has historically been challenged. More than that, such historical narratives of resistance are inspirational and validating for students. To hyper focus on oppression in study of racism and ignore or gloss over resistance to that racism is to reduce the power of antiracist pedagogy. During CTI, we learned to cultivate Black joy by joining into podcasts produced by the *Abolitionist*

Teaching Network, hosted by Bettina Love and Gholdy Muhammed. Zetta Elliott, a well-known children's book author and activist, Zoomed into our seminar one evening to teach us how the artistic movement known as Afrofuturism is salient in her own fictional revisionist histories of Black people. I (Erin) revised a lesson I teach about Japanese prison camps in an undergraduate class to include a simultaneous study of Michi Weglyn, Yuri Kochiyama, and Aiko Herzig-Yoshinaga: Japanese American activist women who were integral figures in the redress movement. What we feel is important to stress here is that, for us, infusing content about race and racism was only as powerful and effective as were our efforts to include content about resistance to racism.

In sum, Kishimoto (2018) suggested that antiracist pedagogy is first characterized by the infusion of content related to race and racism. For us, that meant learning things we were not taught to us in our own schooling experiences. This was critical to our ability to create curricular units for our students. For example, as CTI participant, Anne Galligan, a white woman, spent time learning about activists of Color like Fred Katagiri, Susan La Flesche Picotte, and Osh-Tisch in preparation to plan a unit for her first-grade students on characteristics of heroes. Her school curriculum covered the usual white heroes and token heroes of Color (i.e., Martin Luther King and Rosa Parks), but she understood the importance of learning and teaching more comprehensive and inclusive stories. As she explained, this meant a deep dive into material that was not a part of her K–12 schooling, or her teacher preparation program. Anne read articles detailing the resistance by many lesser-known people of Color. She watched *The Power of an Illusion, White Like Me*, and *The Making of Asian America, 500 Year History*, and *500 Nations*. Anne simultaneously learned about the ways resistance played a part of the stories she unearthed. And, like Kishimoto (2018) outlined in the second characteristic of antiracist pedagogy, how she taught this to her students was as important as what she taught.

Pedagogical Approaches

Kishimoto (2018) wrote that educators have a tendency to treat the infusion of content about race, racism, and antiracism as the "ending rather than entrée point for anti-racist pedagogy" (p. 546). This is erroneous. An analysis of race and power must be organized around the more difficult task of considering appropriate teaching methods. Despite the importance of knowing things, antiracist pedagogy is not simply about incorporation of content related to race, racism, and antiracism. It is about considering and creating new responses to social inequality. This best happens when students and teachers co-construct knowledge together "to afford a theoretical framework capable to informing a rich responsiveness to educational questions" (Thompson, 1997, p. 28). The importance of co-construction of pedagogy cannot be understated as it is an attempt to dismantle asymmetrical power relations between teachers and students. It is important that teachers are not positioned as the sole authorities on the problems, taking control of the policies, programs, and pedagogical practices that are designed to correct them.

Kishimoto (2018) outlined important criteria when considering pedagogy. Teaching in ways that are pedagogically supportive of the development of critical consciousness should include efforts to: (1) challenge assumptions and foster students' critical analytical skills; (2) develop students' awareness of their social positions; (3) decenter authority in the classroom and have students take responsibility for their learning process; (4) empower students and apply theory to practice; and (5) create a sense of community in the classroom through collaborative learning.

With these criteria in mind, it is important that antiracist pedagogy does not hyper focus on the race consciousness of white students because this does not help students of Color (Blackwell, 2010). A pedagogy that "unfolds around white students" (Blackwell, 2020, p. 487) merely rectifies racism. Nor should antiracist pedagogy put students of Color on the spot as brokers for white students figuring out how to engage with antiracist pedagogy. With these cautions in mind, it is also instructive to remember that there is no linear path related to pedagogical approaches: in fact, antiracist pedagogy that is prescriptive or serves as a template is not antiracist.

Avoiding Prescriptive Pedagogy

In CTI, we worked hard to avoid setting our pedagogical plans for the antiracist units of study in stone, heeding the advice from scholars like Zamalin (2019) and Tanner and Miller (2019), who suggested that antiracism must allow for improvisation. Educators should be careful about avoiding "prescriptive and harmful racial scripts" (Tanner & McCloskey, 2022, p. 4) to challenge racism. In an attempt to gain experience co-constructing knowledge with one another through improvisational pedagogy as an example for how that work could be accomplished with students, Dr. Sam Tanner, an improv artist and race scholar, joined our seminar via Zoom one evening. Dr. Tanner taught us that antiracism is best explored in unscripted, generative, and relational ways. Holding what we learned from Dr. Tanner to heart, we left ample spaces in our units for students and teachers to build pedagogical practices in tandem with students. In other words, the units of study were not overly scripted. Rigid scripts, pre-identified "correct" responses, and fixed ways of challenging racism are antithetical to antiracist pedagogy.

Antiracist Pedagogy as Interdisciplinary

Most of what we know about antiracist pedagogy has come from studies in teacher education (Teel, 2014). This led to a major early critique of antiracist pedagogy that it was not interdisciplinary (Dei, 1996). It is true that much of what we studied about antiracist pedagogy came from teacher education; however, antiracist activism has a rich and diverse interdisciplinary history. Our study of antiracist activism that could inspire our pedagogy included art, poetry, and music that challenged racism. When possible, we learned from young people. For example, we followed the work of Malik Norman, a senior photography student at UNCC. For Malik's senior research project, he discovered a local rural community's Black history was lost when the high school in the town was integrated. Norman's project, "Visual Waters," is his attempt to right that wrong and recapture stolen Black histories. His intent with his entire photography practice, he said, "is to educate, agitate or advocate" (Leggett, 2021). Learning about antiracist projects outside of the teaching and teaching education was critical to open windows of opportunity for us in designing effective pedagogy. What is important here is that while our own teaching contexts ranged from general education to discipline specific (biology, history, English), we witnessed the power of interdisciplinary contributions when taking up antiracist pedagogy. This was important too as we considered how to engage our students in antiracist organizing/activism, another central characteristic of antiracist pedagogy.

Antiracist Organizing/Activism

Antiracism refers to a "active resistance" to racism (Thompson, 1997, p. 9). Antiracist pedagogy is fundamentally concerned with exploring new possibilities for racial equity (Dei, 1996). As a curricular project, antiracist pedagogy includes explicit instruction on confronting racism without reservation. Antiracist pedagogy is a pedagogy that seeks to transform society by challenging the individual as well as the structural system that perpetuates racism (Kailin, 2002). Zamalin (2019) insists that antiracism is built on the direct and ongoing confrontation with the philosophy of racism, racists, and the structures of racism, rather than taking on hardened racists. This is important because sensationalizing bad actors only "exonerates the majority of decent people who—despite their awareness—are nonetheless responsible for keeping intact racial inequality" (p. 39).

In CTI, we used essential statements to help us think through the ways our pedagogy could be action-oriented. Essential statements were sentence stems that helped articulate and focus the relationship between racism, antiracism, and pedagogy. For example, we each wrote statements using this sentence stem: "If racism is/looks/sounds _____, and antiracism is/looks/sounds_____, then antiracist pedagogy could challenge racism by _____." This exercise was instructive because it helped us frame antiracist pedagogy as a direct response to racism. A characteristic in each CTI final unit was a focus on activism, an essential characteristic of antiracist pedagogy. For example, Elizabeth Hayes, a high school history teacher, developed a revisionist unit of the civil rights movement. Her students studied first-person accounts from activists who were buried in whitewashed narratives because they were seen as too political, such as Angela Davis and Assata Shakur. As a culminating project, her students were required to research, analyze, and present the traits of activism describing what they did with their feet (where they went), hands (what they did), head (what they thought), mouth (what they said), and heart (what they might have felt or believed). This activity was instrumental in helping the students learn the various ways people can engage in antiracist activism. From this point of departure, the students created their own activist projects.

Teacher Positionality

Undergirding these three components is a teacher's critical reflection on their own social position as a raced being in a racially stratified society (Kishimoto, 2018). In other words, it is possible for a faculty to have an intellectual understanding of power relations and racism, and therefore be able to teach racial content in class, without necessarily applying this analysis to their own social position. Teacher self-reflection on their social position includes understanding that identities are not static (Tatum, 2003), that we possess both privileged and oppressed identities (Hurtado, 1996), and that our socialization and intersecting identities (including internalized racial superiority and internalized racial inferiority) can impact our teaching. Self-identity work is an important part of antiracist pedagogy. This self-reflection requires teachers to have the humility to know that they are a work in progress, both as individuals and as pedagogues. Antiracist pedagogy is not a ready-made product that professors and teachers can simply apply to their courses but, rather, is a process that begins with teachers as individuals, and continues as they apply the antiracist analysis into course content, pedagogy, and their activities and interactions beyond the classroom. Sharing our own vulnerability as well as generating empowering experiences with students can lead to creating a sense of community in the classroom.

I (Angela Walker) am a Black female educator working in a Title I school with a student body composed of 80 percent African American students and 99 percent students of Color. I believed that antiracist pedagogy was what I needed to deconstruct the anti-Black internalized racism I detected in my own thought patterns and belief system. Kohli (2014) defines internalized racism as "a phenomenon that, like racism impacts all communities of color . . . it results in the conscious or unconscious acceptance of a racial hierarchy where the culture, values and beliefs of the dominant culture are prioritized over the culture values and beliefs of racial minorities" (p. 368). Because policies and practices that rely on beliefs of Black criminality, dishonesty, ignorance, unintelligence, and oversexualization pervade every facet of society, I realized that I had internalized anti-Blackness myself. This was important to name and address in CTI because it had the potential to impact the creation of my unit of study.

In our seminar, we devoted time to exploring our own identities as raced people. For example, we wrote *Where I'm From* poems (Lyons, 1999) with an explicit focus on our racialized identities. We used strategies from Singh's (2019) *Racial Healing Handbook* to more deeply examine and process our own racialized stories. We learned about developmental models of racial identity development to bridge theoretical connections to our own personal experiences. All of this work was foundational to our process of enacting antiracist pedagogy with our students. In the chapters that follow, we provide snapshots of our work. Our goal is to be as transparent as possible about our learning goals for our students and the ways we worked toward those through content development, pedagogical practices and activism. We hope that by offering windows into our work, we will demystify what we mean when we used the term antiracist pedagogy.

References

Asante, M. K. (1991). Afrocentric Curriculum. *Educational leadership*, 49(4), 28–31.

Baines, J., Tisdale, C., & Long, S. (2018). *"We've been doing it your way long enough": Choosing the culturally relevant classroom.* Teachers College Press.

Blackwell, D. M. (2010). Sidelines and separate spaces: Making education anti-racist for students of color. *Race, Ethnicity and Education*, 13(4), 473–494. https://doi.org/10.1080/13613324.2010.492135.

Blakeney, A. M. (2005). Antiracist pedagogy: Definition, theory, and professional development. *Journal of Curriculum and Pedagogy, 2*(1), 119–132. https://doi.org/10.1080/15505170.2005.10411532.

Dei, G. (1996). Critical perspectives in antiracism: An introduction. *The Canadian Review of Sociology, 33*(3), 247–267. https://doi.org/10.1111/j.1755-618X.1996.tb02452.xIn.

Dennis, D. (2021, June 1). Clint Smith's book reckons with the lies told about American history. *ANDSCAPE.* https://andscape.com/features/clint-smiths-book-reckons-with-the-lies-told-about-american-history/.

Dillard, C. (2021). *The spirit of our work: Black women teachers (re)member.* Beacon Press.

Du Bois, W. E. B (1973). Whither now and why. In Aptheker, H. (ed.). *The education of black people: Ten critiques, 1906–1960,* 149–158. University of Massachusetts Press.

Fleming, W. C. (2006). Myths and stereotypes about Native Americans: Most non-Indians don't know a great deal about the first peoples of the Americas, Mr. Fleming avers. But what's worse is that much of what they do "know" is wrong. *Phi Delta Kappan, 88*(3), 213–217.

Gay, G. (2010). *Culturally responsive teaching: Theory, research, and praxis.* Teachers College Press.

Hurtado, A. (1996). *The color of privilege: Three blasphemies on race and feminism.* University of Michigan Press.

Kailin, J. (2002). *Antiracist education: From theory to practice.* Rowman & Littlefield.

King, J. E., & Swartz, E. E. (2015). *The Afrocentric praxis of teaching for freedom: Connecting culture to learning.* Routledge.

Kishimoto, K. (2018). Anti-racist pedagogy: From faculty's self-reflection to organizing within and beyond the classroom. *Race Ethnicity and Education, 21*(4), 540–554.

Kohli, R. (2014). Unpacking internalized racism: Teachers of color striving for racially just classrooms. *Race Ethnicity and Education, 17*(3), 367–387.

Ladson-Billings, G. (1995). Toward a theory of culturally relevant pedagogy. *American Educational Research Journal, 32*(3), 465–491.

Ladson-Billings, G. J. (1999). Preparing teachers for diverse student populations: A critical race theory perspective. *Review of Research in Education, 24*(1), 211–247.

Leggett, P. (2021, May 17). UNCC grad breaks out of his comfort zone with photos of his community near Charlotte. *Charlotte Observer.* https://www.charlotteobserver.com.

Love, B. L. (2019). *We want to do more than survive: Abolitionist teaching and the pursuit of educational freedom.* Beacon Press.

Lyon, G. E. (1999). *Where I'm from: Where poems are from.* Absey & Co.

Miller, E. T., & Tanner, S. J. (2019). "There can be no racial improvisation in White supremacy": What we can learn when anti-racist pedagogy fails. *Journal of Curriculum and Pedagogy, 16*(1), 72–96. https://doi.org/10.1080/15505170.2018.1525448.

Morris, M. (2016). *Pushout: The criminalization of Black girls in schools*. The New Press.

Muhammad, G. (2020). *Cultivating genius: An equity framework for culturally and historically responsive literacy*. Scholastic Incorporated.

Nash, K. T., Glover, C. P., & Polson, B. (2020). *Toward culturally sustaining teaching: Early childhood educators honor children with practices for equity and change*. National Council of Teachers of English.

Paris, D., & Alim, H. S. (2014). What are we seeking to sustain through culturally sustaining pedagogy? A loving critique forward. *Harvard Educational Review, 84*(1), 85–100.

Saad, L. F. (2020). *Me and white supremacy: Combat racism, change the world, and become a good ancestor*. Sourcebooks, Inc.

Singh, A. A. (2019). *The racial healing handbook: Practical activities to help you challenge privilege, confront systemic racism, and engage in collective healing*. New Harbinger Publications.

Smith, C. (2021). *How the word is passed: A reckoning with the history of slavery across America*. Little, Brown and Company.

Tanner, S. J., & McCloskey, A. (2022). Improv theater and whiteness in education: A systematic literature review. *Review of Educational Research, 90*(1), 6–23.

Tatum, B. (2003). *Why are all the Black kids sitting together in the cafeteria?*, revised edition. Basic Books.

Teel, K. (2014). Getting out of the left lane: The possibility of white antiracist pedagogy. *Teaching Theology & Religion, 17*(1), 3–26.

Thompson, A. (1997). For: Anti-racist education. *Curriculum Inquiry, 27*(1), 7–44. https://doi.org/10.1111/0362-6784.00035.

Wagner, A. E. (2005). Unsettling the academy: Working through the challenges of anti-racist pedagogy. *Race Ethnicity and Education, 8*(3), 261–275.

Wynter, S. (2003). Unsettling the coloniality of being/power/truth/freedom: Towards the human, after man, its overrepresentation—An argument. *CR (East Lansing, Mich.), 3*(3), 257–337. https://doi.org/10.1353/ncr.2004.0015.

Wynter-Hoyte, K., & Smith, M. (2020). "Hey, Black child. Do you know who you are?" Using African diaspora literacy to humanize blackness in early childhood education. *Journal of Literacy Research, 52*(4), 406–431.

Zamalin, A. (2019). *Antiracism: An introduction*. New York University Press.

CHAPTER TWO

Dismantling Internalized Anti-Black Racism in Literature Instruction through Racial Identity Reflection

Angela V. Walker

> To love all children, we must struggle together to create the schools we are taught to believe are impossible: schools built on justice, love, joy, and anti-racism.
>
> —Bettina Love

"Antiracist" is a popular buzzword in today's educational discourse. It is both a popular trend among those seeking to be allies in response to recent civil unrest and a target of opposition among those who believe that antiracism's theoretical underpinnings are anti-American. Roughly six months before the pandemic shutdown and the release of a presidential memo condemning antiracist diversity education as "un-American" and "propaganda" (Voight, 2020), I excitedly undertook a K–12 teaching fellowship dedicated to defining and implementing antiracist pedagogy. The initial task was to write a curriculum unit that applied antiracist tenets to practical instruction. These resources would be available for other teachers seeking to incorporate antiracist materials into their teaching methods.

As an additional but equally important undertaking, I personally endeavored to understand my own internalized racism as I taught literature to students of Color in a predominantly African American high school. I eagerly accepted both the official challenge to write the curriculum unit and my personal charge to unpack internalized anti-Black racism with the intent of implementing antiracist pedagogy in my twelfth-grade English language arts (ELA) classroom. I positioned myself to explore critically my own process of preparing the curriculum unit, also grounding my reflective process in the following questions: How do the instructional approaches I select for this unit develop students' own awareness of anti-Black internalized racism? How do my own unchecked assumptions of Black inferiority yet pervade the teaching approaches I adopt as well as the daily interactions I have with Black students?

Positionality

As a Black female educator working in a predominately and historically Black school with a student body composed of approximately 80 percent African American students and 99 percent students of Color overall, I believed that antiracist pedagogy was what I needed to deconstruct the anti-Black internalized racism I detected in my own thought patterns and belief system. Kohli (2014) defines internalized racism as "a phenomenon that, like racism impacts all communities of color . . . it results in the conscious or unconscious acceptance of a racial hierarchy where the culture, values and beliefs of the dominant culture are prioritized over the culture, values, and beliefs of racial minorities" (p. 368). Policies and practices that rely on beliefs of Black criminality, dishonesty, ignorance, unintelligence, and oversexualization pervade every facet of society. Unfortunately, the assumption of Black academic, cultural, and behavioral inferiority insidiously persists in majority African American environments, especially schools. These settings are rife with racist discipline policies and instructional practices despite research that shows how teachers of Color provide positive models in their classroom interactions (Egalite et al., 2015). Schools are dualistic environments in which African Americans and other teachers of Color are susceptible to developing "ideas, beliefs, actions and behaviors that support or collude with racism" (Bivens, 2005). For this reason, antiracist teaching is a continual process of becoming that requires immense reflection and adaptation as educators honestly consider and confront the ways that curriculum, school policies, and classroom management reinforce white superiority and whiteness as the default or normal position.

Content about Race and Racism

Classroom discussions immediately prior to the pandemic in the 2019–2020 academic year revealed that my students were wrestling with their own negative racial perceptions, feelings of inferiority, and questions of identity. I was certain that the killings of George Floyd, Breonna Taylor, and Ahmad

Arbery would only bring more questions to bear in the new academic year. Therefore, I felt it appropriate to apply an intersectional lens to my antiracist approach, particularly to the analysis of the texts we read in class.

Coined by legal scholar, Kimberlé Crenshaw, in "Demarginalizing the Intersection of Race and Sex" (1989), intersectionality is a framework for examining and evaluating inequality. It centers conversations about discrimination at the intersection, or the place where the overlap between systems of discrimination occurs, giving multi-marginalized people priority in voicing their experiences in the conversation. Doing so is not meant to divide, as adversaries to antiracist education suggest, but rather it enables the actualization of community by "restructuring and remaking the world where necessary" (p. 167). Remaking the world to be a place of equitable learning and opportunity should be the goal of teachers aiming to create a community of learners that is both inclusive of and affirming of all students irrespective of race/ethnicity, gender, class, ability, and so on. The classroom should be a supportive, safe community where students can inquire, explore, and evolve in their thinking and in practice without the imposition of inferiority.

That said, I was especially excited about the prospect of creating an ELA curriculum unit that addressed racism from the standpoint of anti-Black internalized racism using intersectionality as a guiding framework for first recognizing how race is socially constructed and then dismantling oppressive practices, mindsets, and structures that imposed an inferiority complex on students of Color. The focus on internalized anti-Black racism was due to the reality that anti-Black racism is "the most expansive, historically durable, and salient form of racism" (Zamalin, 2019, p. 7). To address internalized anti-Black racism would to some degree also be beneficial for other students of Color in unpacking internalized oppression from their own cultural contexts. Not only did I hope that students would begin to unpack and reject anti-Black racism in all its forms, but because the unit relied on the concept of stories as the means for understanding others, I also hoped that students would unpack and reject all forms of discrimination as they saw them working in their own lives. As for my own journey, I believed that becoming more attuned to students' understanding of race would reveal shortcomings in my own assumptions.

Pedagogy

According to Blakeney (2005), antiracist pedagogy is "a paradigm located within Critical Theory utilized to explain and counteract the persistence and impact of racism" (p. 119). Antiracist pedagogy is an approach to teaching that extends beyond merely adding racial content and resources into curriculum. It encompasses a critical evaluation of the how of instruction even when race is not the central concept being explored, and it incorporates an analysis of how socialization and intersecting identities influence approaches to instruction. A significant feature of antiracist pedagogy is introspection, or the requirement for educators to reflect upon and to critically examine their positionality, taking note of how their positional lens influences their decision making in the classroom (Kishimoto, 2018). The ability of teachers to reflect on their social environment, and their position in it, is essential to engaging crucial conversations about race and racism, bringing to bear a constant sensitivity to and critique of their practice (Ladson-Billings, 1996).

During the 2021–2022 academic year, the second year of teaching this unit, I engaged the curriculum with thirty-seven high school seniors in three separate sections of an advanced literature course meant to enhance students' critical reading, writing, and interpretation skills. The unit spanned ten class sessions, which were instructed face-to-face on an alternating A/B-day format. The total instructional time for each block was ninety minutes. Students examined literary concepts such as character, setting, structure, perspective, and figurative language. They were instructed to articulate and to evaluate how writers effectively use language to create new meaning, to foster purpose, and to reflect the dynamics of society as the writers themselves perceive it.

I chose William Shakespeare's play *Othello* as the anchor text through which students would demonstrate these competencies. I believed it to be relevant due to themes related to race, racism, miscegenation, suicide, and sexism. The play's titular character is a highly revered general of African descent who marries a young, white Venetian woman named Desdemona, the daughter of a senator. As news of Othello and Desdemona's elopement spreads throughout the community, Othello becomes the target of derogatory language, deception, and accusation. He also wrestles with notions of his own inferiority, blaming his wife's supposed infidelity on his own blackness. Due to the treacherous manipulation of Iago, the main villain of the play, Othello murders Desdemona, erroneously believing that she has been unfaithful. He learns the truth of her fidelity shortly after murdering her, and in response he dies by suicide (Shakespeare, n.d.).

Given the complexity of the text and the ideas presented therein, I was certain that *Othello* would generate robust conversation about the complexity of race and humans' preconceived notions of one another. My goal was not to force students to believe one way or the other. I assumed that students, with the proper tools and a carefully fostered environment, could thoughtfully apply antiracist thought and intersectionality to their analysis of *Othello*.

Throughout the process of reading, responding, and reflecting, students gathered evidence from *Othello* to support their perception of his character, his motives, his intent, and his insecurities. In their analyses, students were to explain examples of both internal and external conflicts that emerged ultimately leading to Othello's demise. Internal conflict also included interpretations of internalized anti-Black racism.

To initiate the process of dismantling anti-Black racism (including its internalized manifestation), students needed to develop an understanding of how race has been constructed and has evolved over time. I assigned supplementary texts from diverse genres to employ a multifaceted approach to conceiving race and to assist students in building a framework with which to engage the sensitive subjects we would discuss. The supplementary resources included historical texts, poetry, and popular antiracist books. Of particular note, Ibram Kendi's (2017) *Stamped from the Beginning: The Definitive History of Racist Ideas in America* was available in an audio version at no cost to students. I assigned portions of it to establish the definition of racism as any practice or idea that assumes one group is inferior to another. Racism, according to Kendi, is a "collection of racist policies that lead to racial inequity" (p. 20). These racial inequities are justified and reinforced by a series of racist ideas such as segregation and assimilation, ideas predicated upon the acceptance of white superiority. Racist ideas are detrimental to people of Color because they make people of Color think less of themselves, thus making people of Color more vulnerable to racist ideas.

Another antiracist text that was useful in grounding classroom discussion was Ijeoma Oluo's (2019) *So You Want to Talk about Race*. This book provided a straightforward, accessible description of how racism and racial oppression systematically appears in today's school systems. Oluo is particularly adept at explaining the school to prison pipeline and the resentments students of Color harbor while at school. Oluo's examination of the astronomical numbers of Black and Brown youth who are pushed from public school systems into the prison system resonated with some of the stories I had heard from students in the past regarding friends and family who were ensnared by the disciplinary cycle of consequences, suspension, and confinement.

To ensure that students placed William Shakespeare and *Othello* in their proper contexts, I devoted the first three lessons of the curriculum unit to background, also gauging students' initial understanding of British literature and iterating important points about Shakespearean society. I highlighted the common elements of Shakespeare's plays, explaining the general differences between comedies, tragedies, and histories. The lessons also emphasized the ways that Shakespeare departed from the tradition of his time in his approach to characterization and structure.

Most of the instructional time in the lesson was devoted to introducing the concept of the tragic hero and his characterization, though I also spoke of the presence of Africans in London by the time that *Othello* was first performed in 1604. As a warmup activity for the third lesson, I directed students to respond in writing to the following question: "Based on the background information shared last period, how do you think Shakespeare's *Othello* challenged or supported racial stereotype in those days?" To prepare students for an informed response, I pointed out to the class that the first Black actor, F. W. Aldridge, did not play Othello until May 1825. All actors playing Othello in years prior did so in blackface, and that the overall attitude toward Africans in London at the time of the original performance was one of fear and distrust (Shaw & Shaw, 1995). Though scholars debate whether blackface or other performance practices can be honestly evaluated as racist according to historical standards, reading *Othello* from the standpoint of a Black person in contemporary Western society adds nuance and allows perspectives to emerge that would otherwise be invisible (Thompson & Smith, 2016).

On a different occasion, the class and I analyzed Othello as a complex character of Color in leadership by introducing themes of mask-wearing. As the warmup activity, students discussed practices that forced them to wear a public face, or a "professional" persona, hiding the trauma that racism and internalized racism imposes. As the guiding texts for this discussion, students analyzed Paul Laurence Dunbar's "We Wear the Mask" (1896) and Maya Angelou's adaptation of Dunbar's poem "The Mask" (1987). Subjects that emerged from the discussion included code switching, talking "proper," and dealing with microaggressions. In response to laments about having to adapt speech and language, students affirmed personal beliefs that the African American Vernacular English (AAVE) and code switching were both respectable and necessary elements in the Black experience. However, students believed they were empowered most when they themselves determined how and when to use these different languages as opposed to being forced to use them only in certain settings.

The remaining lessons in the unit focused on student experiences as expressed in their journals. For ten days, students wrote journal entries expressing their thoughts about *Othello* and the background readings. The purpose of the journal entries was for students to examine closely how they thought or felt about themselves in relationship to the world, and to examine how those perceptions affected their interpretation of literature. I provided students with the following four guidelines for writing their journal entries and several guiding questions to direct their writing if they experienced writer's block:

Guidelines

1. Open with a claim or a clear position that comes to mind when reading the guiding questions.
2. Use vocabulary from supporting readings (i.e., anti-racist, assimilationist, segregationists, divergences, etc.) to explain your thoughts and positions.
3. Refer to the guiding questions below to direct your thoughts should you get stuck.
4. Explain, explain, explain.

Guiding Questions

1. How do you define your identity?
2. When were you first made aware of the idea of race?
3. Who has helped to shape your understanding of your identity?
4. In what ways do different identities intersect?
5. Select a character from *Othello*. What does the dialogue in the play reveal about your character's racial attitudes? Gender attitudes?
6. How do your character's actions reflect ideas from some of our other texts such as "We Wear the Mask" (Dunbar), *Stamped from the Beginning*, and/or Maya Angelou's mask poem?
7. How would you describe your own position on racism, sexism, poverty, and other types of discrimination in the world?
8. At this point, do you think that Othello is a racist play? Why/why not?

Reflections on Racial Identity

Every assignment I give includes a model students can use to generate thought. I shared the following entry from my journal as the model:

> Identity is a complex idea that covers more than race. It has taken me a long time to define mine, but now I can say with clear understanding that I am a CIS gendered Black woman who has learned to love her Blackness and her womanhood. I used to question why I was different, and there have been many times that I tried to be something else other than who I am. I tried to assimilate

because I believed that people outside my poor, predominantly Black/Latinx community would accept me if I learned to fit in. Yes, I was an assimilationist. I thought that the idea of the United States as the "great melting pot" meant that we would all just learn to blend our cultures. I learned the hard way that I was expected to erase my idea of Blackness in order to embrace someone else's way, a way that assumed whiteness as the perfect ideal.

I first became aware of my race in kindergarten when I realized the "flesh" colored crayons in my crayon box weren't the color of my flesh. Later on in elementary school, I learned a new word to describe my discomfort: racist. One day my teacher, an older white gentleman who constantly told us about his German heritage, told me that the smell of my hair oil made him sick to his stomach. It smelled like coconuts, and he said that he hated coconut. He suggested that I tell my mother to buy a different kind. When I went home that evening, I shared with my mother the things my teacher said. She immediately responded with, "He is racist." I did not quite understand what "racist" meant, but I knew it was not a good thing. Over the course of that school year, I was put in remedial classes. My teacher directly told me that I was destined for pregnancy and welfare. That year, I earned the lowest grades of all my entire elementary school years.

Students' journal entries were incredibly insightful. The information provided will help me adapt the unit for future years. First, most students wrote about the complexity of their identity, how navigating it is exhausting. This recurring idea has signaled the need for incorporating additional resources for social and emotional support in the classroom. The support provided should be attuned to the experience of dealing with racism as well as other forms of discrimination that may coincide with it.

To demonstrate the need for incorporating social emotional resources that are culturally tailored for students of Color, I present the journal responses of three students, N. T., M. B., and A. T. The first student, N. T., contends the following regarding intersecting identities:

> Best way for me to explain is like a soda machine that has all the sodas mixed into one cup. That is how my identity intersects with one another; each flavor of soda represents a part of my identity. Sometimes that cup can get over filled and fizz over. Some of these flavors of soda can conflict with one another. That can be overwhelming for that cup. Sometimes parts of my identity can overwhelm me and it can make me feel burnt out. On those days I don't feel like doing anything, I just want to lay in my bed and just not exist anymore. But on sunny days I feel like I picked the right soda and be productive.

When referring to racial awareness and how racial identity can be confusing because assumptions are often based on appearances, M. B. observes:

> The first time I was made aware of the idea of race was when I was in middle school. I began to realize that people hung in groups, the black people hung with the black people, the white people hung with the white people, etc. I didn't belong in a group. I was labeled "too white" for the black kids and "too black" for the white kids. It also didn't help that everyone would call me white, or ask what I'm mixed with. It was a very confusing time for me.

The third student, A. T., emphasizes the ways that discriminatory stereotypes are perpetually recycled, underscoring the need for more intentionality in addressing stereotype at the beginning of the year as the classroom culture is being established. Addressing stereotype is not just a one- or two-class activity. It should be emphasized consistently over the duration of the class until the original thought patterns are subverted. The following statement from A. T. brings this point to the forefront:

> I feel like the discrimination in this world is never going to stop. The ideologies that culture and ignorance pushed in previous years will always make its way around, whether the person knows it or not. I feel like everyone is guilty of perpetuating stereotypes or participating in microaggressions.

A. T. highlights the reality that discrimination is culturally embedded, and people often unknowingly participate in it. For this reason, A. T. does not have much hope that discrimination can be eradicated. Despite the belief that racism and other forms of discrimination is reinforced through culture, A. T. also does not believe that Shakespeare perpetuated racism in *Othello*. The parts that can be deemed racist are merely a reflection of the time as A. T. contends in the following in response to the question of whether *Othello* is a racist play:

> I do not feel like Othello is a racist play. I think it portrays how microaggressions work and that some people will act friendly to your face and make fun of your race behind your back. Of course it has some racist parts. But, people have to realize what time period this was in. This was a time where black people were looked down upon and seen as property. Everyone isn't going to look at Othello as a war hero but merely a black man that thinks he has power. If no one had anything to say about Othello's race, it would most likely be deemed as unrealistic.

A. T.'s assessment of *Othello* stands in contrast to M. B.'s perception of the play. M. B. does not distinguish between parts of the play versus the whole, but emphatically states that it is racist, arguing,

> Othello was a weak minded protagonist that had problems with internalized racism. Iago was greedy, and I don't like greedy people. He was clever though and I do enjoy a competent person. . . . Was Othello a racist play? Yes it was. At the very beginning they were yelling about Othello being with Desdemona and using racial slurs to stir up Desdemona's father. Othello obviously didn't like his own race the way he led himself. He wanted to fit in according to what everyone else said.

What both A. T. and M. B. demonstrate in their differing conclusions is that students can agree on their experiences with racial discrimination, but they can differ in their perceptions of what is or is not racist. This highlights how slippery the idea of racism is. If it is not clearly defined and the involved parties agree on the definition, those involved in identifying it will come to different conclusions on what it is, further complicating efforts to dismantle it.

Conclusion

The varied perspectives of students have greatly informed my own. I am enormously grateful for the insights that students shared, and all the ways that I was challenged to expand my understanding of race. I was able to identify shortcomings in my own thinking, and I engage the process of dispelling and dismantling my own biases with each day in the classroom. However, I cannot help but to feel as though little has changed since I first taught the unit in November 2020.

My discomfort with the progress in antiracist teaching is not a reflection on my students. The process of unpacking internalized racism has magnified for me the systemic shortcomings of public education. The system is grossly flawed. It does not adequately measure student achievement or teacher effectiveness, especially among Black students. To create an environment where Black students and other students of Color can thrive, alternative forms of evaluating teacher performance and student achievement must be developed. Otherwise, all attempts to include resources and perspectives from communities of Color will only be additive approaches.

References

Angelou, M. (2017, February 7). We wear the mask. [Video]. YouTube. https://www.youtube.com/watch?v=_HLol9InMlc&t=15s.

Bivens, D. K. (2005). What Is Internalized Racism? In Potapchuk, M., Leiderman, S., Bivens, D., & Major, B. (eds.), *Flipping the script: White privilege and community building* (pp. 43–51). MP Associates, Inc., and the Center for Assessment and Policy Development (CAPD).

Blakeney, A. M. (2005). Antiracist pedagogy: Definition, theory, and professional development. *Journal of Curriculum and Pedagogy*, 2(1), 119–132.

Crenshaw, K. (1989). Demarginalizing the intersection of race and sex: A black feminist critique of antidiscrimination doctrine, feminist theory and antiracist politics. *University of Chicago Legal Forum*, 139–167.

Egalite, A. J., Kisida, B., & Winters, M. A. (2015). Representation in the classroom: The effect of own-race teachers on student achievement. *Economics of Education Review*, 45, 44–52.

Kendi, I. X. (2017). *Stamped from the beginning: The definitive history of racist ideas in America*. Random House.

Kishimoto, K. (2018). Anti-racist pedagogy: From faculty's self-reflection to organizing within and beyond the classroom. *Race Ethnicity and Education*, 21(4), 540–554.

Kohli, R. (2014). Unpacking internalized racism: Teachers of color striving for racially just classrooms. *Race Ethnicity and Education*, 17(3), 367–387.

Ladson-Billings, G. (1996). Silences as weapons: Challenges of a Black professor teaching White students. *Theory into Practice* 35(2), 79–85.

Love, B. L. (2019, March 18). Dear White teachers: You can't love your Black students if you don't know them. *Education Week*. https://www.edweek.org/teaching-learning/opinion-dear-white-teachers-you-cant-love-your-black-students-if-you-dont-know-them/2019/03.

Oluo, I. (2019). *So you want to talk about race*. Seal Press.

Shaw, R., & Shaw, R. (1995). "Othello" and race relations in Elizabethan England. *Journal of African American Men*, 1(1), 83–91.

Shakespeare, W. (n.d.) *Othello* (B. Mowat, P. Werstine, M. Poston, & R. Niles, eds.). Folger Shakespeare Library. https://shakespeare.folger.edu/shakespeares-works/othello/.

Thompson, A., & Smith, I. (Experts). (June 14, 2016). Teach him how to tell my story [Audio podcast]. Folger Shakespeare Library. https://www.folger.edu/shakespeare-unlimited/othello-blackface.

Vought, R. (2020). Memorandum for the heads of executive departments and agencies. (Report No. M-20-34). Executive Office of the President: Office of Management and Budget. https://www.whitehouse.gov/wp-content/uploads/2020/09/M-20-34.pdf.

Zamalin, A. (2019). *Antiracism: An introduction*. New York University Press.

CHAPTER THREE

Justice Is More Important Than Kindness

Antiracist Pedagogy in a First-Grade Classroom

Anne Galligan

"What do you notice about this picture?" I asked my first-grade class while analyzing a painting of the Second Continental Congress one afternoon in May. A white girl raised her hand and said, "It's all white people. And boys." With a perplexed look on his face, a Latino student asked, "Why is there all white people?" Another student, an Asian boy, responded with his thoughts: "Maybe [people of Color] were invited but they did not want to come." A Latina challenged this: "I think they were not allowed to come. I think they only let white boys come because George Washington is a white boy." A Black boy indicated his agreement: "I agree. He doesn't like Brown people; he wants to keep the Brown people at home." To which a Black girl said, "That's not fair. That was mean. That's when white people did not like Black people. People need to be treated like they want to be treated and it's not fair that Black people get treated mean and white people get treated nice." A Black girl, who thought the people in the picture were meeting to pick a president, said, "That's not fair. Black people should get to pick the president too. If you don't let them pick, maybe there would never be a Black president. Presidents are special and all, but not if they don't play fair. If they don't play fair, they don't respect people and presidents should respect people." A Latina chimed in with her agreement: "Girls should be there. There should be Indigenous and Black people and people with all Color skin. That's just not nice."

As the conversation unfolded, my role as the teacher was to ensure each student had a chance to share uninterrupted. Later, I would address misconceptions. But, for the moment, I simply listened. It was powerful to hear young students lead a challenging conversation and make sense of systemic racism in the context of what they already understood about white supremacy. Their ability to agree and disagree while adding their own perspective came from months of practice—months of being encouraged to use their voice and challenge or question information frequently. In just a few minutes, the students demonstrated a deeper understanding of systemic racism than many people would have believed possible of first graders. The students of Color were not distraught and the white students were not being shamed or feeling shameful. Collectively, they had a calm, frank conversation about fairness, a topic often covered in elementary classrooms, only this time in the context of racism.

Background and Positionality

In the description of my teaching above, my goal was to teach a multidisciplinary unit on "hidden heroes," or figures usually not recognized as national leaders despite their tireless efforts in antiracist activism. Before I could begin to prepare for a unit like this, it was important that I did some critical reflection on my own upbringing. As a white child raised in a white home in a white community in a predominantly white school during a period when color-blindness was considered by white people as politically correct, my racial identity development was a slow process; oftentimes, it was completely stagnant. No one acknowledged my race, explained to me that conforming to white norms made me complicit in racism, or guided me to question the injustices resulting from the social construction of race. I was simply taught to be a good girl and treat everyone fairly. I was under the impression, for a very long time, that if I was merely kind and respectful to all people, I was not implicated in racism.

For most of my life, I subconsciously saw white people as the norm and people of Color as a deviation from that norm. Even through high school, my understanding of racism was limited to overt, hateful, and intentional harm and discrimination. I had been led to believe that this definition was the all-encompassing definition of racism and that racism, by this definition, was largely a thing of the past, except for rare instances from the Deep South. I thought that what I viewed as "serious" racism—racism in systems, policies, and practices—had been eradicated after the civil rights movement. While some of this was based on my own ignorance, this was explicitly taught to me during thirteen years of whitewashed curricula in schools. I was entirely disconnected from the issues of racism and did not acknowledge race, racism, racial formation, or the power relations surrounding races. Even through college, I did not yet understand the powerful grip that white supremacy had on education and other systems.

If I am not careful, I could act based on the default mentality I was socialized into as a child, allowing the status quo to continue harming Black and Brown people, including those in my classroom. The insidious and unrelenting hold of white supremacy on the systems and institutions within this country led to my slow, and often stagnant, racial identity development. These are merely snippets of the power whiteness has had in my life and how I have been complicit in maintaining it in my own life and in the lives of others. Having had the opportunity to further my education and intellectual growth has loosened the grip of white supremacy ever so slightly and has allowed me to be more aware of and resistant to it.

The Infusion of Content

For this unit, I was committed to infusing content related to race and racism in age-appropriate ways that began with an in-depth study of the excellence and resilience of people from marginalized groups whose heroism was exemplified through their fights for racial justice. I knew that such positive affirmations for my students was essential to the development of strong and positive racial identity (Love, 2019; Muhammed, 2020). To educate myself, I spent countless hours during my own research before I designed a first-grade curricular unit built from the ideas of antiracist pedagogy.

In my first-grade classroom, a standard unit of study is on national holidays. Since the traditional unit focuses on significant people—"heroes"—who have been honored by holidays, such as Christopher Columbus, George Washington, Thomas Jefferson, Abraham Lincoln, and Martin Luther King Jr., I wanted to modify the unit to expose my students to heroes of Color whose significant contributions had not been nationally recognized nor honored with holidays.

I wanted to show my students the genius of people of Color, as well as how people of Color have used heroic acts to work toward racial justice. We learned about heroes from diverse racial identity groups including Malcom X, Ruby Bridges, John Lewis, Juan Felipe Hererra, Cesar Chavez, Joan Baez, Fred Korematsu, Reverend Mineo Katagiri, Joy Harjo, Susan La Flesche Picotte, and Osh-Tisch. I chose these heroes to intentionally showcase people with a variety of racialized and gendered identities who represented a diverse age spectrum. To show students that resistance is not an endeavor of the past, I paired historical figures with present-day activists to show that resisting oppression is an ongoing, ever-present struggle.

I wanted my students to see themselves and their friends within these leaders. When I introduced Fred Katagiri, an Asian American man, I put his picture on the board, as I did with each leader. Immediately, one of my Asian students, typically reserved, raised both of his arms in the air with excitement and declared "Yay! He looks like me! I hope he is a hero because he looks like me." His peer, an African American girl, responded, "That's so cool that he looks like you!"

For my students, seeing an Asian American in the context of resistance and brilliance, as opposed to someone who is blamed for the world-wide pandemic (COVID-19), was a crucial aspect of interrupting the negative messages students frequently receive about the Asian American Pacific Islander (AAPI) community. For an Asian American student, who has had to contend with the fact that the stories of people who "look like" him have been mis- or unrepresented in his classrooms previously, simply seeing a member of the AAPI community on the screen sparked pure joy and excitement.

My teaching of this unit situated myself as a learner alongside my students. Prior to this unit, I had rudimentary knowledge about Malcom X, Ruby Bridges, and Cesar Chavez, but the other figures were unknown to me—a product of my own whitewashed curriculum in K–12 schools. To learn enough to infuse content related to race and racism in my unit, I reviewed a great deal of literature and research. I knew that not only did I need to learn the facts about both nationally recognized white heroes and unrepresented heroes of Color, but I also needed a deeper understanding of white supremacy and its vicious role in America's history and the presentation of historical narratives. And most important, I needed a better understanding of the rich history of Black, Asian, Indigenous, and Latinx peoples in the United States, outside of the context of marginalization and oppression. I read articles detailing the resistance by many less-known people of Color. I watched *The Power of an Illusion*, *White Like Me*, *The Making of Asian America*, *500 Year History*, and *500 Nations*. I listened to *A Talk to Teachers*. This list is not comprehensive but is a glimpse of the sources that had the greatest impact on the creation of this unit.

Practices

When we began our unit, we started with pre-assessments that would allow me to better understand my students' perception of "heroes." In the pre-assessment, the students were asked to imagine a hero, draw what they visualized, and write to describe what makes someone a hero. Every student, without fail, imagined a superhero, and wrote about their superpowers. Some of the students described well-known fictional superheroes, and others created their own make-believe superhero. Most of my students created white superheroes. Once the students shared their preconceived notions about heroes, we worked together to create a list of criteria required to declare someone a hero. The students, although having described heroic magical powers in their papers, created a list that did not include superpowers. Instead, they listed: "To be a hero one must: help people, do good things, stop bad guys, not hurt good guys, and fix problems." We used this checklist each time we learned about a leader, those nationally accepted as leaders and those unrecognized, and decided if they should be honored as a hero. This began our path of thinking critically about the whitewashed messages society and schools push about key figures in history and today.

To analyze the nationally recognized leaders, including Christopher Columbus, George Washington, Abraham Lincoln, and Martin Luther King Jr., the students were presented with information from multiple perspectives. Once the students had read the dominant narrative about these figures and a narrative from the point of view of people of Color, they were given the liberty to decide if they considered each figure a hero or not. Considering the information presented in the different perspectives were quite contradictory, we discussed the power structures present that led to white narratives being widely accepted as truth while the truthful narratives of minoritized groups are hidden.

While learning about Christopher Columbus, the students were shocked to hear the ways he harmed Indigenous people. In the dominant version of the story, the author we read de-emphasized the violence against Indigenous peoples and, instead, described Columbus's role as merely bringing goods and "Indians" back to Europe with him. After reading this section, we paused and discussed what the author meant by the description. One student said, "People who are heroes don't do that!"

In another lesson, I taught students about George Washington and discussed the fact, often erased from history lessons, that he enslaved hundreds of African people. The students questioned why people think someone who "traps" Black people at his house is a hero. A student declared, "That sounds like a villain to me." Students began to delineate the difference between a hero and a villain while questioning why some figures of history are lionized and their actions sanitized.

While these were not the only actions carried out by the men we discussed, they were the ones that garnered the most significant responses by the students. In their critical analysis of the picture book texts that the students studied, they questioned the label "hero." They wondered how a person who carries out acts of violence, trauma, and genocide could ever be labeled a "hero." In doing this critical work, students learned to read about those figures of history with a more discerning eye, question the dominant narratives, and parse out truths from untruths. As consumers of text, they began at a young age to triangulate sources of information, study the narratives being told, and learn *how* to question and challenge the narratives that are presented throughout schooling.

The work of students reading and questioning critically is not a finite process. This work requires the spiraling of the curriculum, where each year students can return to this work, examine other powerful advocates and activists of Color and advocate for learning about other figures whose stories have not been widely shared.

The lessons that centered leaders of Color gained the active engagement and excitement of my students. While the students had been exposed to fictional people of Color in picture books all year, centering and learning about *real* people of Color daily, outside of their respective "history months," seemed to be the most powerful for the students. The students wanted to hear "awesome" stories about what people with the same racialized identity they possess have done throughout history. I presented the actions of each leader, encouraged students to analyze their actions in relation to the unjust white supremacist power structures in existence, and allowed the students to discuss amongst themselves whether that person was a hero or not (See figure 3.1).

The students discussed how Ruby Bridges's parents wanted her to go to school that had more resources because the white people in power did not let the resources go to schools with Black children. They talked about how Malcom X demanded that Black people have power and protection. The students discussed that even though Cesar Chavez witnessed injustice, he was brave to organize protests that improved the lives of many Latinx people. As they learned about Joan Baez, a Latinx folk singer, they were amazed how she used her talented singing voice to resist oppression. The students had not considered that one way to speak back to white supremacy was through our artistic talents. Since many of them had an interest in singing, they decided that would be a way they would like to push back against white supremacy too. Students decided that "heroes" were those who had the courage, bravery, and generosity to resist oppression. While this is not a comprehensive list of the students' reactions to the leaders of Color we learned about, it demonstrates their early understanding of resistance and their interest in following in the steps of their "heroes." The students, even at a young age, already un-

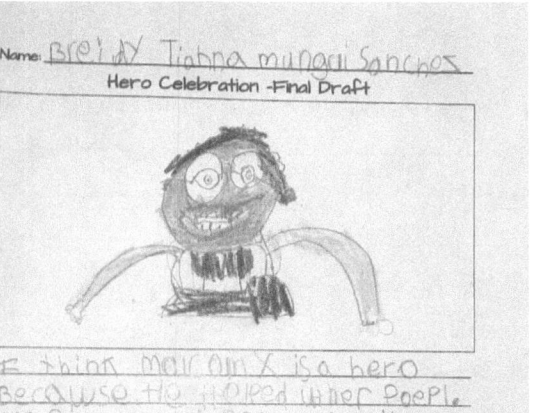

"I think Malcom X is a hero because he helped other people to protest because White people had all the power and Black people didn't have no power. Malcom X used his voice. He was a hero for many reasons."

Figure 3.1. Hero Celebration Final Draft. Source: Anne Galligan

derstood that bravery is not the absence of fear, but it is one's actions despite being afraid. One student specifically indicated this understanding with the statement: "[To stand up for yourself] you can be brave. You can breathe out and in if you are scared."

Active Resistance to Racism

The students indicated their understanding of resistance while writing persuasive pieces about which of the leaders of Color they would like to honor and why. They also indicated their empowerment by creating puppets of themselves as "heroes" and writing how they would use each body part of the puppet to resist and/or fight the oppression of peoples of Color. (See figure 3.2.)

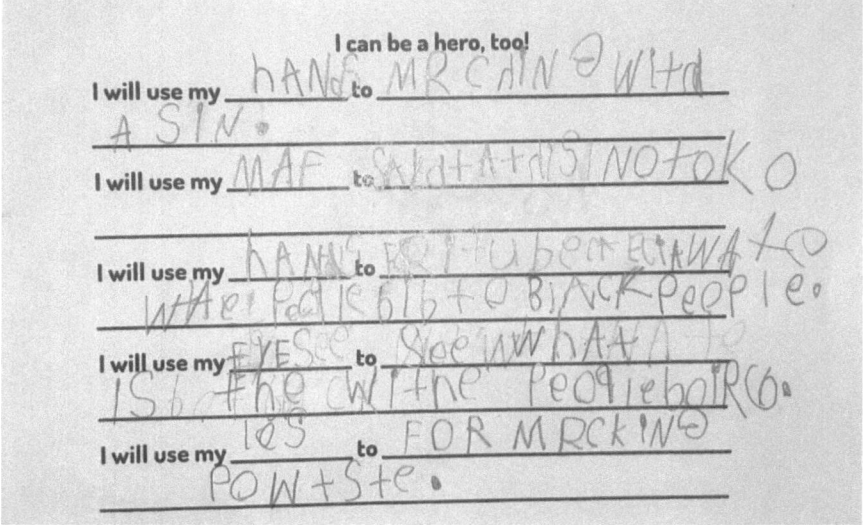

"*I will use my hands to marching with a sign.
I will use my mouth to say that's not okay.
I will use my hands for writing because I see what White people did to Black people.
I will use my eyes to see what is the White people doing.
I will use my legs for marching [in] protest.*"

Figure 3.2. I can be a hero, too! Source: Anne Galligan

In their work, they demonstrated that they would use their voices, some indicated "at the top of their lungs," to tell people in power "that's not right" when witnessing or experiencing injustice. Through role play, they practiced their loud voices and giggled at the newness of raising their voice in a classroom; while they created deeper understanding through play, I watched in awe. These empowered six- and seven-year-old students may not have completely understood the profoundness of their determination to assert their rights and take up space in a country that actively demands the exact opposite of them, but I did.

Conclusion

My classroom was a space of art, not propaganda. I was not interested in indoctrinating my students into a political agenda, something that antiracist teachers have been accused of doing as backlash pedagogy (Gutiérrez et al., 2002). Quite the contrary, I was committed to teaching my students to challenge and question what seems obvious by offering them multiple perspectives and asking them to meaningfully take up some of the most provocative questions of our time including questions about fairness, justice, and opportunity—all essential inquiries in a democracy. As Thompson (1997) reminds us, "Democratic education IS anti-racist education" (p. 17).

At the end of my unit, when my students were asked if *they* were heroes, a resounding "yes" was heard. Each one of them was able to share with pride how they were already heroes and how they could be heroes for the rest of their lives. For young students, heroism is often attributed to others, seen as an inherent magical trait they do not possess, or something they must wait until they are adults to achieve. Through the intentional inclusion of leaders of Color resisting racism in curricula, the explicit interruption of racist messaging, the fostering of critical thinking skills, and my constant critical self-reflection, the students were empowered to see themselves as their own heroes. By the end of the unit, my students had a deeper understanding of heroism. One did not have to have superpowers; one simply had to resist or interrupt injustice in small or big ways. With that understanding, the students declared that anyone, of any gender identity, race, or age, could be a hero. This explicitly included themselves.

References

Gutiérrez, K. D., Asato, J., Santos, M., & Gotanda, N. (2002). Backlash pedagogy: Language and culture and the politics of reform. *The Review of Education, Pedagogy & Cultural Studies, 24*(2), 335–351.

Love, B. L. (2019). *We want to do more than survive: Abolitionist teaching and the pursuit of educational freedom.* Beacon Press.

Muhammad, G. (2020). *Cultivating genius: An equity framework for culturally and historically responsive literacy.* Scholastic Incorporated.

Thompson, A. (1997). For: Anti-racist education. *Curriculum Inquiry, 27*(1), 7–44. https://doi.org/10.1111/0362-6784.00035.

CHAPTER FOUR

Middle School English Language Arts

My Personal Story of Exploration, Empowerment, and Antiracist Teaching

Seun Omitoogun

On August 9, 2014, I was eagerly anticipating my first-year move-in day at the University of North Carolina at Chapel Hill where I hoped to learn to be a middle school teacher. On that same day, Michael Brown Jr.'s life was cut drastically short by police officer Darren Wilson in Ferguson, Missouri. At this point in my life, I did not have the proper words or understanding to articulate my professional passion to address racism through my teaching. I had just begun to truly develop an understanding of my own racial identity development. As a soon to be first year college student, I was just in search of a better understanding of my role in society. But on August 9, 2014, I knew I had an opportunity that Michael Brown Jr. would never have. I felt obligated to use my educational opportunity to pursue a career inspired by the transformative change I dreamed of. This reflection guided my journey toward antiracist education. To me, antiracism in education is specifically addressing different conscious and unconscious racially oppressive structures in curriculum and school cultures. This is necessary because the perpetuation of the power from whiteness is harmful for us all. Stakeholders in the education system must be actively working to be antiracist by unlearning, rethinking, and at times challenging what has been upheld as the norm. Without this active response, I believe individuals run the risk of contributing to the continued perpetuation of racism. It has been critical to recognize the personal responsibility of this task, but it is equally as imperative to understand the impact is greater when there is collective efficacy.

The pedagogical unit described in this chapter was my attempt during the 2018 to 2022 school years to construct a four-part, year-long antiracist curriculum for my seventh grade English language arts students. The curriculum covers four broader themes: identity, history of racism, contemporary social justice, and activism to empower students with an academic toolkit to be agents of change.

Critical Reflections: Who Am I to This Work?

My racial identity is an incredibly important aspect of what makes me who I am. It is the topic that drives my professional aspirations. And, as a function of authentic antiracist work, my intersectional identity as a Nigerian American cisgender woman shapes much of my understanding and experiences navigating conversations about race. Access to educational opportunities transformed my life outcomes as a second-generation immigrant. This realization and reflection is a critical lens within which I approach my practice. In *The Succeeders: How Immigrant Youth Are Transforming What It Means to Belong in America*, Flores (2021) describes similar academic achievements of immigrant students and explains "this striving toward success, they believe, shows them to be the exceptions to the moralized and race-based rules of belonging" (p. 109). This describes my experiences navigating the K–12 public education system as a younger person.

Despite the diversity within the United States, I believe that individual people are more alike than different. By listening to individual stories, I was able to deepen my personal development while simultaneously expanding my perspective. I believe these critical reflective practices and community-driven learning are the keys to transformative change in education. There is power within lived experiences; therefore, there is power in learning about and finding value in each of our individual stories. I come to this work with multiple identities and lived experiences that combine together to influence my pedagogical approach and practices.

In order to dive deeply into antiracist pedagogy and co-construct it with my colleagues and students, I had to spend time prioritizing, reflecting, and better understanding my racial identity. Understanding my racial story more deeply strengthens my work as an antiracist educator. My personal racial identity development journey impacted my ability to teach and empower a diverse population of learners. Critical reflection about my racial identity challenged me to prioritize healing within myself. This is essential to being a better version of myself and for authentically supporting the growth of others.

What I Learned to Develop the Curriculum

Though transformative teaching requires personal work, teachers need pedagogical tools as well. I was able to find extremely helpful teaching resources online. *Learning for Justice* (https://www.learningforjustice.org) was an impactful, free online resource I used for lesson ideas and curriculum planning. The website offers complete lessons and activities aligned with social justice standards. Building an antiracist curriculum is a constant learning journey of deepening my personal knowledge and then applying it to my pedagogy. *Learning for Justice* is special because the website offers resources for all parts of the journey. The website is user-friendly and allows for teachers to customize their materials for individual curriculum needs. I also did a lot of Google searches of themes and found several individual assignments or mini-units that I integrated into my year-long curriculum.

Furthermore, I leaned into community expertise to better support my professional development through this journey. Community organizations that supported my professional development included the *Black Genius Profile* created by *Village of Wisdom* (https://www.villageofwisdom.org/pledge-to-protect-black-genius) and *Working to Extend Antiracist Education* (https://www.weare-nc.org). *The Black Genius* provides a theoretical framework that was useful in helping me decide on broader culturally-affirming, social justice elements that my curriculum needed to address. It provided me with five concrete elements to ground my thinking about what needs to be incorporated into each lesson, which strengthened my pedagogical practices. *The Black Genius* elements provided me with a theoretical toolkit that supported building relationships with students and families; these relationships were critical for creating a stronger classroom community. *Working to Extend Antiracist Education* (https://www.weare-nc.org) provided me with a supportive community of educators actively thinking about and engaging in the intentional implementation of antiracist pedagogy with students as young as rising first graders.

The Curriculum

To develop my curriculum, I started with a guiding question. My seventh-grade classes explored the question: "What do we, as Central Park seventh graders, need to develop and sustain a healthy community?" In the first quarter of the year, we focused on what are the elements of individual identity and how those identities influence the lived experiences individually and collectively as a school community. This is intentionally designed to "connect in school learning with out of school living" as well as "create community among individuals of different cultural, social, and ethnic backgrounds" (Gay, 2013, p. 49). Navigating conversations about these topics in a multicultural space with students who possess varying degrees of theoretical understanding and vocabulary of those various identities revealed for me the complex intersections of how race and other elements of student's identities manifest in teaching and learning. The purpose behind beginning the school year with the broader themes of identity and community is to build trust as a class. The students focus on sharing their own lived experiences, and reflecting on important elements of what makes them who they are.

In the second nine weeks, the curriculum transitioned to a history of racism through the use of excerpts from the powerful story *The Narrative of the Life of Frederick Douglass* (Douglass, 2014) as the central text. The students explored the historical context that Douglass was writing in and his purpose as an abolitionist and proponent of change. Students looked at primary sources, articles, poetry, and graphic novels to better support their understanding of an above-grade level rigorous text. Figure 4.1 is a photograph of a student reading a chapter from *The Life of Frederick Douglass: A Graphic Narrative of a Slave's Journey from Bondage to Freedom* by David Walker (2019). I downloaded this chapter from *Engage New York* (https://www.engageny.org) to facilitate a deeper understanding of the central text. In fact, several of the resources I used within this unit came from *Engage New York*, which is free and available online.

Our deep exploration of Frederick Douglass created a historical context for students to draw contemporary connections around how systemic racism persists into the present day. Using the central text, *The Hate U Give*, by Angie Thomas (2017), my classes discussed topics of systemic racism, code-switching, the power of language, and activism. One of my favorite parts of *The Hate U Give* are the explicit connections to the world that my students are living in. To supplement this, we analyzed the Ten Point Program of the Black Panther Party and Black Lives Matter Movement. These primary sources added depth to student learning by giving them context for the reading, world around them, and practice analyzing their own opinions.

As a connection to *The Hate U Give* and the world around them, several lessons focused on music videos, song lyrics, and the stories that the musicians tell through these pieces. Some examples include "Changes" by Tupac, "Be Free" by J. Cole, "Bigger Picture" by 'Lil Baby, and "I Can't Breathe" by H.E.R. The most powerful moments for me personally have always been each student's personal journey in their ability to grapple with, analyze, and self-

Middle School English Language Arts ~ 43

Figure 4.1. Photograph of Student Reading Supplemental Graphic Novel. Source: Seun Omitoogun

facilitate discussions about complex contemporary issues of social justice, in a way that many adults struggle with. To culminate the unit, students shared their major takeaways. Figure 4.2 is a photograph of one student's final reflection. Figure 4.3 is a portion of the same student's final writing project in which students wrote about the specific core values that guide their own lives as it connected to the pedagogical theme of activism covered in the unit. Student responses like these reaffirmed my belief that antiracist work in education requires us to radically reimagine, innovate, and transform systems for more liberatory outcomes.

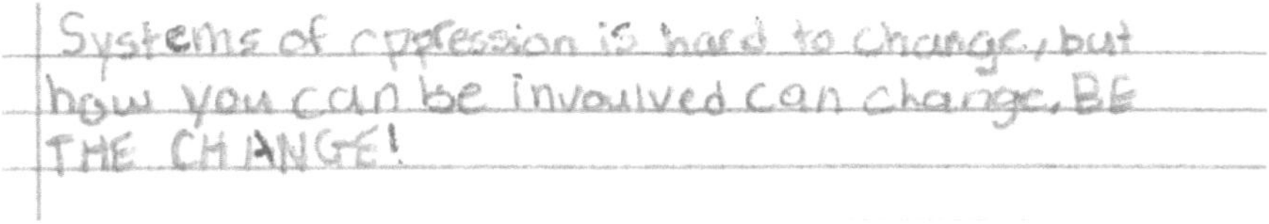

> Systems of oppression is hard to change, but how you can be involved can change. BE THE CHANGE!

"Systems of oppression is hard to change, but how you can be involved can change. BE THE CHANGE!"

Figure 4.2. An excerpt by Anika describes her final takeaway from "The Hate U Give."
Source: Seun Omitoogun

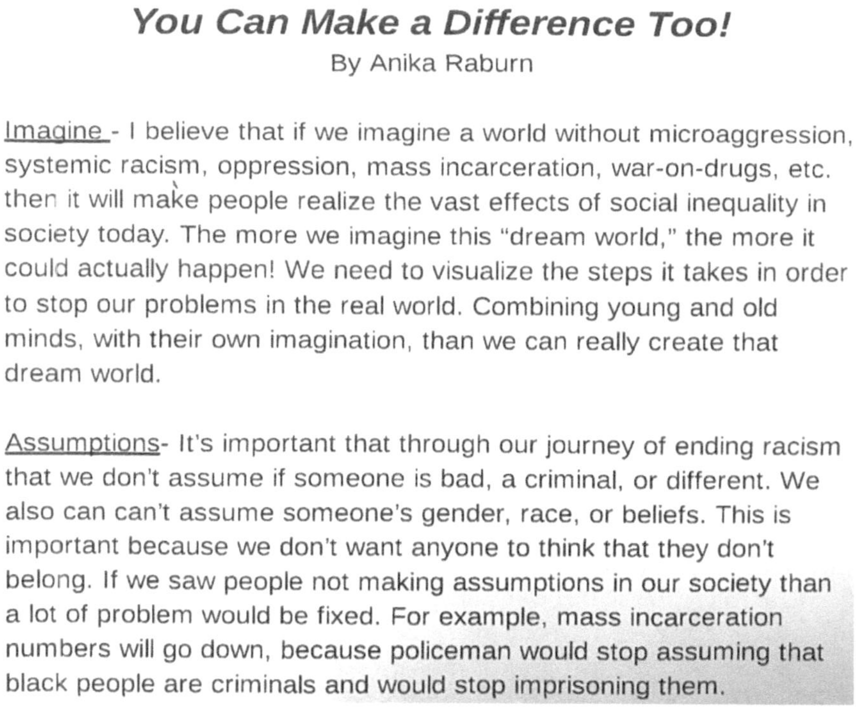

You Can Make a Difference Too!
By Anika Raburn

Imagine - I believe that if we imagine a world without microaggression, systemic racism, oppression, mass incarceration, war-on-drugs, etc. then it will make people realize the vast effects of social inequality in society today. The more we imagine this "dream world," the more it could actually happen! We need to visualize the steps it takes in order to stop our problems in the real world. Combining young and old minds, with their own imagination, than we can really create that dream world.

Assumptions- It's important that through our journey of ending racism that we don't assume if someone is bad, a criminal, or different. We also can can't assume someone's gender, race, or beliefs. This is important because we don't want anyone to think that they don't belong. If we saw people not making assumptions in our society than a lot of problem would be fixed. For example, mass incarceration numbers will go down, because policeman would stop assuming that black people are criminals and would stop imprisoning them.

Figure 4.3. Example of a Student's Final Writing Project. Source: Seun Omitoogun

Action

The final nine weeks of the school year are spent thinking about the word "action." The entire school year builds a contextual framework for students to be able to grapple with the question: "What are the core beliefs that guide individual student's lives?" Furthermore, students reflected on areas they see a need for change and concrete ideas for how they can push against historically dominant systems. One example of student activism that came in the final part of the year was a student group named "The Hate We Get" after the central text. The student group collectively organized to identify and challenge systemic barriers in our school community. Figure 4.4 is a list of demands from "The Hate We Get" student group, which are similar in structure to the Ten Point Program of the Black Panther Party.

- We want Diversity in our classrooms and in school!
- We want more knowledge on our heritage and people of color.
- We want respect in/out of school.
- We want to be treated equally.
- People of Color's history needs to be recognized all year.

Figure 4.4. List of Demands from Student Group. Source: Seun Omitoogun

Furthermore, students produced powerful pieces that highlight their deep understanding of the content and the world around them. Student reflection about their biggest takeaways from the curriculum highlights that antiracist teaching is not indoctrination; rather, it is exposing students to rehumanizing content and introducing them to experiences to navigate real world challenges.

Reflections

The Importance of Relationships with Families

Throughout this learning process, it was incredibly important to build relationships with families through transparent communication. I was the most successful when I consistently engaged families and welcomed them into the learning process. It was important to be clear and transparent with families about the learning intention and assignments because of the sensitive nature of the content; however, I also stressed the importance of being adaptable and open minded in order to approach this learning journey in a care-driven way. This required me to be extremely prepared and organized as an educator. For example, during the unit on *The Hate U Give*, I provided parents with a week-by-week syllabus (see figure 4.5) covering assigned chapters, themes, and activities utilized in class. Processes like the aforementioned gave me an opportunity to co-construct curriculum with parents and invite them to be involved in their child's learning journey.

The book at a glance

Due to the sensitive nature of the book's themes within our current society, we want to emphasize that we take it very seriously that our class discussions and reflections are thorough and care driven. Therefore, we want to let you all know that the scheduling is flexible, to allow us time to have detailed and in depth class conversations and individual reflection, without rushing material that students will need time to process. **We will never move ahead of the listed schedule, but there is the chance that we might move slower than the information provided to give students more processing time.** Below you will find a tentative, week by week list of topics, themes, and discussions we will have with the novel.

Week of	Chapters to be read	Themes/Topics in class
1/18-1/21	1, 2, (provided by school if students do not have books yet)	Norms around classroom discussion Language as a intentional choice/ cultural difference Police brutality- a nationwide problem
1/24-1/28	3, 4, 5, 6	Author's Purpose Police brutality- a nationwide problem Character tracking Chapter summaries Double Entry Journals Quiz on chapters 1-6
1/31-2/4	7, 8, 9	Police brutality- a nationwide problem Dueling identities and code-switching Socratic Seminar
2/7-2/11	10, 11, 12	Dueling identities Power of community -why do people protest? Why do acts of protest turn violent? Stereotypes and language (the power of things you say)/ microaggressions Socratic seminar

2/14-2/18	13, 14, 15, 16	Cycle of poverty and racism
		   -13th clips related to Maverick's lesson
		Stereotypes and language (the power of things you say)/ microaggressions
		Power of community and activism
		   -what does activism look like as a middle school student?
		   -Individual and large group reflection
		Socratic Seminar

2/22-2/25	17, 18, 19, 20	Cycle of poverty and racism Power of community and activism Character development (static vs. dynamic characters)

Figure 4.5. Week-by-Week Syllabus. Source: Seun Omitoogun

Navigating White Fragility

In *Learning for Justice's* (formerly named *Teaching Tolerance*) (Teaching Tolerance, 2019) interview with Robin DiAngelo, DiAngelo discusses how whiteness and its responses (fragility) can act as barriers to race work in the education community. She explains the good/bad binary of individual racism that has created a pattern of defensiveness for white people who feel the need to defend their moral character, as opposed to understand the root causes of structural racism. The term fragility describes how easily white people can deflect uncomfortable conversation about race, intentionally and unintentionally, through actions such as crying. Similar barriers to antiracist growth showed up in my own experiences. These directly disrupted my implementation of antiracist pedagogy, but through critical self-reflection, I was able to heal enough to move past the traumatizing aspects of these barriers and gain a deeper understanding of the urgency of antiracist practices.

For example, my very first year implementing this curriculum, I received escalatory pushback to the implementation of *The Hate U Give* unit. I vividly remember walking into the school excited about the lesson I was going to teach that day—my classes were analyzing the Ten Point Program to build context around Big Mav, a character in *The Hate U Give*. Less than ten minutes into the school day, a coworker gave me a heads up about the gossip within the school's parent network.

The gossip was about me and how several parents were unhappy about the book choice. The parents in this situation demanded a response from the executive director of the school and threatened to go above him to the state level. I remember the devastation I felt. I had planned, I had communicated, I had innovated. Because of the work I had put in, I struggled with such a negative response to my hard work. It was difficult for me to recognize that more people supported the curriculum than those who were opposed. The response and display of power from the parents who were opposed to the curriculum illustrates an example of white fragility I faced as an educator of Color.

Upon learning about the parent's reactions, I cried on the phone with the school's executive director as I questioned whether I wanted to go forward with the curriculum. Though I ultimately found the personal strength to move forward with antiracist pedagogical unit, this experience directly impacted my self-perception as a Black educator teaching in a multicultural setting. I had to push back on personal thoughts and feelings of being unworthy and incapable of teaching this antiracist curriculum in a care-driven way. These thoughts directly stemmed from my interactions with this small group of parents. One of the ways I dealt with my own insecurities was to respond decisively, yet professionally, to concerned parents. For example, I respectfully explained my pedagogy to a parent who requested a meeting with me, the middle school director, and the executive director of the school. In an email response (see figure 4.6) to her request, I wrote, "In this current system we live in, Tamir [Rice] was not too young to learn this life-ending lesson [about police brutality], so there is no reason to think our students at Central Park are too young to learn it either."

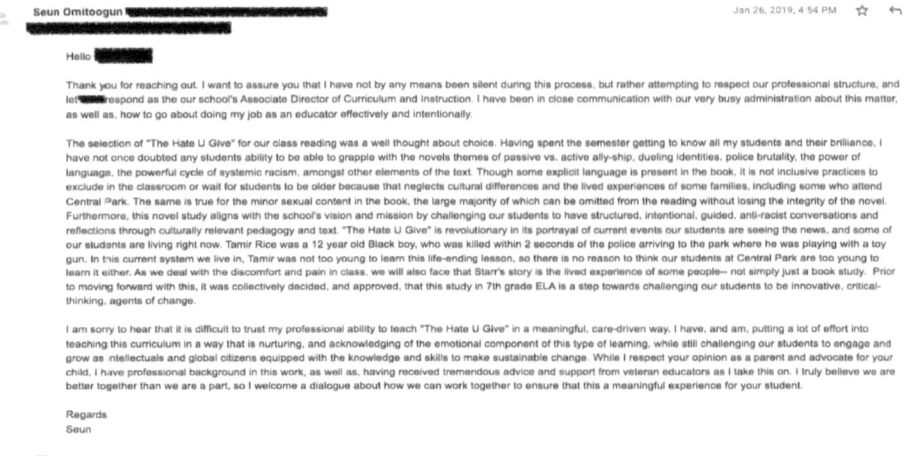

Figure 4.6. Screenshot of Response to Escalatory Parent Pushback. Source: Seun Omitoogun

Further Implications: Context Matters

Despite these incidents with white fragility, I intentionally sought to work at a school with a mission and vision that aligned with my own personal beliefs. Central Park School for Children's (CPSC) mission, along with their multi-year "All Children Thriving" action plan provided a flexible, supportive network of colleagues, administrators, and families to fully invest in antiracist teaching. While all those things are amazing and supportive of first-year teachers, I learned very quickly in my first year that I couldn't teach everything. As a person who wholeheartedly commits to all that I do, it was difficult for me when I realized that content for class is seemingly endless, but time in class is not. It was even harder trying to narrow down which concepts, activities, and discussions I would need to prioritize within my antiracist curriculum (which ironically, takes up more time). In order to engage in antiracist pedagogy, I needed to learn how to differentiate, prioritize, and blend rigorous learning, high standards, cultural responsiveness, and empathy into each lesson. Rigorous, high standards are necessary to disrupt the dominant narrative and equip students with the skills they need to challenge the narrative themselves. Culturally responsive pedagogy is necessary to be most effective in reaching diverse populations of students and facilitating accessible learning experiences. Finding ways to incorporate empathy is necessary in order to focus on human value. These are the principles I think should be at the heart of the learning all students receive.

Conclusion

While creating a curriculum intended to challenge and disrupt traditional approaches to teaching, I learned I needed to simultaneously challenge school-wide structures to be most effective in my work. The student outcomes in the classroom, my antiracist pedagogy, and personal-professional development paralleled in growth over time. These experiences influenced (and at times, interfered with) my antiracist pedagogy, but each had teachable implications for moving antiracist work forward in action. Over my teaching career, I have witnessed how antiracist practices result in transformative student outcomes. My antiracist practices blossomed into a school-wide exploration of the driving question: What are the strategies, tools, and resources that educators need to grow their hearts and minds to embrace antiracist change? As I continue to learn in my own journey, I believe it is important for all educators to engage in critical reflection about their own identity and how it impacts the ways we all show up differently for each other and for our students. This would go a long way in supporting fellow educators through this humanizing experience. This also aligns with my own racial identity development and the personal growth needed to embrace and incorporate antiracist practices.

As applied to curriculum and instruction, Milner et al. (2019) explains "effective instruction requires that both students and teachers engage in critical reflective practices" (p. 57). I have found this to be foundational in my own journey. I believe fellow educators must reflect intentionally and thoughtfully, or it will interfere with their ability to approach their pedagogical practices with an antiracist lens. Benson and Fiarman (2020) explain that "addressing unconscious racial bias requires constant grappling with a paradox. The work is urgent yet requires patience" (p. 163). Kishimoto (2018) elaborates that the most effective antiracist pedagogical approaches recognize "the faculty's awareness and self-reflection of their social position is important in implementing antiracist pedagogy in the teaching, research, and university/community work" (p. 542). While these are intensive, emotional steps, these practices will be critical to creating school environments and a society where all children can thrive.

References

Benson, T. A., & Fiarman, S. E. (2020). *Unconscious bias in schools: A developmental approach to exploring race and racism.* Harvard Education Press.

Douglass, F. (2014). *Narrative of the life of Frederick Douglass: An american slave.* First Avenue Editions.

Flores, A. (2021). *The succeeders: How immigrant youth are transforming what it means to belong in America.* University of California Press.

Gay, G. (2013). Teaching to and through cultural diversity. *Curriculum Inquiry,* 43(1), 48–70. https://doi.org/10.1111/curi.12002.

Kishimoto, K. (2018). Anti-racist pedagogy: From faculty's self-reflection to organizing within and beyond the classroom. *Race Ethnicity and Education,* 21(4), 540–554.

Milner, H. R., Cunningham, H. B., Delale-O'Connor, L., & Kestenberg, E. G. (2019). *"These kids are out of control": Why we must reimagine "classroom management" for equity.* Corwin.

Teaching Tolerance. (2019, June 11). Teaching Tolerance Interviews Robin Di'Angelo: Author of White Fragility [YouTube]. https://www.youtube.com/watch?v=KCxNjdewAAA.

Thomas, A. (2017). *The hate u give.* Gyldendal A/S.

Walker, D. F. (2019). *The life of Frederick Douglass: A graphic narrative of a slave's journey from bondage to freedom.* Ten Speed Press.

CHAPTER FIVE

Confronting Scientific Racism and Eugenics in a Freshman Biology Course

Pablo Chialvo

> The best available scientific evidence suggests that modern humans do not have biological races (consistent with definitions used for other species), while the best sociological evidence suggests that American racism is still a serious problem affecting the lives of Americans. It is imperative that we disentangle these concepts, because without doing so, it will be far more difficult to make strides toward producing a truly equitable society.
>
> —Joseph Graves Jr.

Although my personality and demeanor has changed dramatically over the course of thirty-one years—from being the shyest kid in primary school to lecturing in front of hundreds of college students—one aspect remained largely the same: my reluctance to engage with the topics of race and racism. Growing up in the suburbs of Farragut, Tennessee, my exposure to non-white individuals was quite limited; looking back through old classroom photos (grades kindergarten to fifth), I found only six classmates who had noticeably darker skin than my own. Had you asked me at the time what made us different, I likely would have said that they were Black, Hispanic, or Asian, and that I, in contrast, was Argentine. Ethnicity, not race, defined my primary identity (Katz & Ivey, 1977). The events of September 11, 2001, fundamentally changed that perspective. Seeing the mistreatment of the very few Arab students at my school, I truly became aware for the first time that: (1) I was white and had the privileges associated with that label; (2) racism against non-whites did, in fact, exist, and; (3) I potentially could be hurting these individuals through my language or social interactions. However, I did not feel like I could do anything about it, lest I become the target for animosity. Given my generally shy nature at the time, I chose to do nothing, to instead "retreat back into the predictability of white culture" (Helms, 1984, p. 156). Though my understanding of white identity did change over the next few decades, my silence did not. For one reason (read: excuse) or another, I failed to make the transition from "not openly racist" to antiracist.

The murder of George Floyd on May 25, 2020, broke me from my silence. I could no longer sit back, comfortable in the social, racial, and cultural cocoon that I had weaved myself since childhood, and simply ignore what was becoming all the more apparent, all the more abhorrent. As protests erupted across the country, I sat down at my desk and searched for ways to educate myself on race and antiracist activism. Of course, I found the popular works of Ibram X. Kendi (2019), Layla Saad (2020), and countless others, but I also discovered the University of North Carolina at Charlotte's graduate certificate program in antiracism. Given my position at Appalachian State, I knew the university would waive tuition costs for classes taken at any UNC system school. I had a plan. I put in my application that week and, thankfully, was accepted to the program. Over the course of the next two years, I learned an incredible amount regarding the history and psychology of racism, racial identity development, race in schooling, and antiracist activism. Such information, however, is powerless without action. As such, I sought ways to incorporate what I had learned into my freshman biology courses for non-majors. After much deliberation, I finally settled on a two-part unit regarding the pseudoscience of race and eugenics.

Learning the Content

Given my relatively insulated upbringing and lack of exposure to scientific theories regarding race or eugenics, I knew putting together such a lesson, even for non-majors, would require an enormous amount of preparation and study. Thankfully, my graduate courses gave me the appropriate framework to organize my thoughts and pursue such information in a structured fashion. I poured over dozens of articles ranging in subject from the historical, philosophical, and scientific underpinnings of race to the development of the American eugenics movement; I scoured the university library for books on human genetics and the psychology of discrimination. While a complete bibliography cannot be included here, I strongly recommend the following books for an (accessible) overview of both race science and eugenics:

- *Superior: The Return of Race Science* (Saini, 2019)
- *The Myth of Race: The Troubling Persistence of an Unscientific Idea* (Sussman, 2014)
- *How to Argue with a Racist: What Our Genes Do (and Don't) Say about Human Differences* (Rutherford, 2020)
- *Racism Not Race: Answers to Common Questions* (Graves & Goodman, 2022)
- *Imbeciles: The Supreme Court, Eugenics, and the Sterilization of Carrie Buck* (Cohen, 2017)
- *A Century of Eugenics: From the Indiana Experiment to the Human Genome Era* (Lombardo, 2011)

Putting It into Practice

In order to have a healthy discussion regarding race (or any sensitive topic), it is critical to not only have the proper background knowledge, but also a clear understanding of the audience. A lesson such as this would be substantially different if I taught freshman biology majors, and even more so in a class of primarily upperclassmen, for instance. As a general education course, my BIO1201 (Biology in Society I) section attracts students from across campus and, thus, is fairly representative of the university as a whole. According to data from AppState's Institutional Research, Assessment, and Planning Office, the majority of enrolled students as of fall 2021 were white (81 percent) North Carolinians (92 percent) from urban areas (65 percent). This information would assist me in choosing examples or stories that students would be familiar with, as well as identify and introduce perspectives that they may not have heard before.

Preparation for this lesson began well before any discussion of race or eugenics; it began the first day of class when the all 218 students sat down in the auditorium to hear what they would be learning about that semester. After a brief introduction about the structure and content of the course, I laid out explicit guidelines or expectations for class conduct, particularly in regards to discussion of sensitive topics (e.g., addiction, mental health, race). I emphasized the importance of creating an inclusive environment that is open and respectful, one in which all students feel comfortable voicing their unique perspectives. The most impactful science, I note, is driven by diverse groups of individuals (Hofstra et al., 2020). Discussions were further facilitated by the use of classroom response systems to collect and display opinions, as well as allow shy students to speak anonymously (PollEverywhere and Mentimeter, respectively). Over the course of fourteen weeks, students became accustomed to utilizing both systems; by the time our discussion of race and eugenics finally arrived, they were comfortable with the uncomfortable.

Perhaps more importantly, though, students understood why we were discussing race in a biology course at all. Too often we hear (especially from politicians) that scientists should "stick to the science" and not discuss topics like race, suggesting that the two are unrelated. This is simply not true. As such, throughout my course, I included examples of how biology (and more broadly, science) has impacted BIPOC individuals/communities. A presentation on cellular division and cancer, for instance, is punctuated by the story of Henrietta Lacks, a Black woman whose cells were taken without prior consent and developed into one of the most widely-used tools in modern medical research (HeLa cells; Skloot 2010). A lesson on disease transmission begins with the story of how anti-Asian stereotypes worsened a bubonic plague outbreak in San Francisco at the turn of the twentieth century (Randall, 2019). The intersection of race and science very much exists, and to ignore it leaves historically marginalized populations at risk of further exploitation or harm.

The Lesson

The day of the first lesson, I took a few moments to remind students of our shared expectations regarding discussions and provide a disclaimer regarding the content we were about to see. Given the recent public outcry surrounding critical race theory (CRT) and its supposed anti-American views, I felt it necessary to distinguish between it (an academic and legal framework used to understand how systemic racism influences society) and the lesson at hand (an overview of race science and eugenics). While the two certainly share some basic commonalities in terms of content, they are fundamentally different in scope, organization, and purpose. As such, they should not be conflated with one another.

I then posed a simple question: why is it difficult to discuss race? After some brief reluctance, several students raised their hands and provided their opinions. "There's a lot of uncomfortable history surrounding race, slavery and segregation and all that," suggested one student. "It's taboo," said another. "It's one of those things that we know exists, that we know means something, but we don't like to acknowledge it." When asked whether they had discussed race in other classes before, only a small group of social work majors raised their hands. Even their American history classes don't adequately cover the subject (SPLC, 2018). Given this hesitance, I noted, it is important that we have such a discussion, particularly given the reality of racism in our country and how racist ideas are grounded in pseudoscience.

The lesson continued. I introduced the historical, philosophical, and scientific factors that contributed to the initial development of race as a biological category, paying particular attention to Linnaeus's classification of man, biological essentialism, the Great Chain of Being, and Biblical explanations of race (e.g., the curse of Ham). "When you look at all this information, what does it seem to point to?" I asked the class. "A racial hierarchy," suggested one student. Even without clear evidence or "proof," many scientists were leaning toward a classification scheme that not only separated races based on questionable attributes, but ranked them from the most civilized to the most barbaric, the most divine to the most bestial. Such pseudoscientific arguments for racial divisions would be strengthened by the rise of physical anthropology during the nineteenth century. The work of such scientists as Louis Agassiz, Samuel George Morton, Josiah Nott, and George Gliddon ("the four horsemen of craniometry"; Graves & Goodman, 2022) gave racist beliefs quantifiable data, hard numbers that supposedly proved the inferiority of non-white individuals. In fact, upon his death, Morton would be eulogized, "for aiding most materially in giving to the negro his true position as an inferior race" (Gibbs, 1851). It was here that I paused to make sure that the students were not overwhelmed. It is totally fine to feel uncomfortable, I reminded them, provided that you don't shut down or become defensive as a result. Several students, either verbally or through the anonymous response system, noted that they were not necessarily overwhelmed by the content itself, but rather the sheer "absurdity" of the evidence put forth to support the existence of racial divisions. Another student found it discomforting that verses from Genesis, a book they had read dozens of times, could be used in such a decidedly un-Christian manner.

We then shifted focus from physical differences to a more evolutionary perspective. The publication of Darwin's *On the Origin of Species* (1859) and *The Descent of Man* (1871) fundamentally changed the discussion of races and their evolution, though in conflicting ways. While Darwin strongly supported the idea of man's common biological origin (monogenism) and the unity of all races under one species, he also predicted that the "civilized" races would wipe out and eventually replace the more "savage" ones. In combination with the work of Herbert Spencer (originator of the phrase "survival of the fittest"; 1864) and others, the concept of social Darwinism began to take shape. Social Darwinism posits that inequalities are entirely natural, as those who succeed in life (e.g., those who are wealthy, influential, or civilized) are inherently more fit for a modern society compared to those who are not. As a result, assisting these "lesser" individuals is unnatural from a biological perspective, and, moreover, could pose a threat to the progression of mankind. Pointing to an open survey slide, I asked, "What could such a theory be used to justify?" The students' responses were both accurate and disturbing: slavery, colonialism, imperialism, and genocide. We ended the class period by discussing, "The White Man's Burden," a political cartoon portraying John Bull (Britain) and Uncle Sam (US) carrying the BIPOC inhabitants of their respective colonies away from savagery and toward civilization (Gillam, 1899). As one student pointed out, such cartoons not only promoted biological essentialism and social Darwinism, but portrayed whites as the "saviors" of those less fortunate, suggesting that colonialism actually benefited native populations.

The lesson continued two days later with a quote by Francis Galton, a cousin of Charles Darwin. After reading *On the Origin of Species*, Galton became fascinated with the idea of heredity, specifically whether intelligence could be passed down through the generations in a similar manner as physical traits. Through extensive quantitative research of influential families in Britain, he concluded that intelligence was, in fact, heritable and that the environment played only a minor role in its development. Moreover, he claimed,

> If a twentieth part of the cost and pains were spent in measures of improvement of the human race that is spent on the improvement of the breeds of horses and cattle, what a galaxy of genius might we not create! We might introduce prophets and high priests of civilization into the world, as surely as we can propagate idiots by mating *crétins*. Men and women of the present day are, to those we might hope to bring into existence, what the pariah dogs of the streets of an Eastern town are to our own highly-bred varieties. (Galton, 1865, pp. 165–166)

In essence, individuals with desirable traits (e.g., intelligence, athleticism, etc.) would be encouraged to breed, thus improving the average human "stock" over time. Galton would label this form of selective breeding in human's positive eugenics. Other scientists, however, viewed this approach as insufficient given that less desirable individuals greatly outnumbered the truly exemplary ones. The solution, of course, was to simply prevent those with undesirable physical, mental, or moral traits (e.g., alcoholism, "feeble-mindedness," promiscuity, etc.) from breeding at all. Negative eugenics, as it would later be known, took several legislative forms within the United States at the turn of the twentieth century, including anti-immigration laws (banning undesirable individuals from entering the country), anti-miscegenation laws (banning interracial marriage and, thus, maintaining racial hygiene), and involuntary sterilization laws.

The latter would be the main focus of our discussion regarding negative eugenics, as I found students were generally less familiar with the practice. In fact, they could not believe that such procedures had ever been conducted. The story of Carrie Buck, her forced sterilization, and the Supreme Court case that ultimately found the operation constitutional (*Buck v. Bell*, 1927) produced visible disbelief and anger in the students. How could anyone, much less a chief justice, claim that sterilization was a "lesser sacrifice," one that improved both her welfare and that of society? Given the abhorrent nature of the decision, why has it never been explicitly overturned? Unfortunately, due to time constraints, I had to move the discussion forward, though the students would have an additional opportunity to engage with the idea of forced sterilizations in a future assignment (see below).

We ended the lesson by looking at more recent examples of race science and eugenics, paying special attention to how they embody many of the same assumptions as older theories. Perhaps the most infamous case is that of *The Bell Curve* (Hernstein & Murray, 1994), which produced a media frenzy at the time of publication and left scientists scrambling to control the damage (Goldberger & Manski, 1995). In it, the authors present data to suggest, among other things, that the average IQ of African Americans is one standard deviation lower than white Americans and, moreover, such differences could not be attributed to socioeconomic factors (income, education, etc.) Rather, they claim, intelligence is primarily influenced by genetics. Such an essentialist viewpoint harkens back to arguments made centuries before regarding the inherent differences between races, arguments that (still) support a very clear agenda: "the continuation of a political economic system that maintains . . . the African American in a position of undevelopment, thus depressing their genetic potential, health, and cognitive performance" (Graves & Johnson, 1995). Though products of completely different times, such claims are consistently structured around the, "same belief in Black inferiority" (Cooper, 2005).

The field of genetics has advanced significantly since the publication of *The Bell Curve* and has elucidated—at a molecular level—our common humanity. However, such progress has also come with the tools and techniques to further build divisions under the guise of science. For instance, bioinformatic analyses such as genome wide association studies (GWAS) allow scientists to find gene variants that are statistically associated with certain traits, typically diseases. The approach has also been used to suggest genetic determinants of educational attainment (Okbay et al., 2022), income (Hill et al., 2019), attractiveness (Hu et al. 2019), and same-sex behavior (Ganna et al., 2019). While there are certainly explicit limitations and caveats to such studies, it is quite easy to simply ignore or not be aware of them, particularly if the information is conveyed through a secondary source such as social media. As we saw with the COVID pandemic and subsequent vaccine rollout, disinformation can spread at an alarming rate and have significant medical, economic, and political consequences (Chou et al., 2022; Muhammed & Mathew, 2022). Misinterpretation of genetic methods is particularly worrisome, as the data can be used to support centuries-old notions of biological essentialism, a cornerstone of racial science. Sadly, such concern is not merely hypothetical. At the time of writing (May 2022), we as a nation are grappling with the aftermath of yet another mass shooting at the hands of a white supremacist. Within his 180-page manifesto, the Buffalo supermarket gunman not only detailed a hateful ideology but also supported his views with figures and data from scientific studies on human genetics (e.g., Viding & Frith, 2006; Witherspoon et al., 2007; Li et al., 2008; Davies et al., 2011; Plomin & Deary, 2015). As I warned my students prior to this tragedy, the underlying assumptions and principles of racist pseudoscience are not new, simply resilient; they are capable of shifting, adapting to new methods as they are developed to uphold a racial hierarchy that does not exist.

Assignment and Samples of Student Work

Following our discussion, I asked students to watch *The State of Eugenics* (Shapiro, 2017), a documentary detailing the forty-four-year history of North Carolina's eugenics board and the legislative fight to provide reparations for the victims of involuntary sterilization. Students then completed a short writing assignment in which they provided four facts they did not know prior to watching the video, three facts they did know, a two-paragraph summary (four hundred words minimum), and one lingering question they had after considering the documentary and the material we had discussed in class. Below are some examples of student questions; the selections highlight several common themes or perspectives, including:

The inadequacy and lateness of reparations.
"How is money ever going to compensate what these survivors suffered? How and why is this always the solution? Why is money the solution to settle such despicable issues? Although this does not undo what the survivors experienced, does it help them move past this or compensate for the life they could have had?" —student V. B.
"Why did it take so long to compensate those who were sterilized by the state? Or at least realize that these people deserved compensation? Why was there even a question about compensating victims?" —student S. B.

Preventing similar events or policies in the future.
"How can we work to prevent this sort of policy from taking root and repeating itself in our government?" —student M. M.
"If a horrific program like this was so widely accepted and popularized despite being grossly immoral and unjust, what does that say about the potential for something similar to happen again? What if something hugely widespread and championed across the country today is just as terrible, but everyone is just too blind to see it or too afraid to speak out against it? We need to regularly reevaluate our belief system as a country, because if something like this happened once, it could happen again." —student A. F.

Having never heard of the North Carolina eugenics program.
"Why is none of this taught in history classes during high school? If we pretend things didn't happen then similar things are bound to happen again. We need to know our history (as a state) so that we understand and value the lives we get to live now."—student D. C.
"As a person who grew up in Mecklenburg County, why did I just learn about this tragedy as a freshman in college when it happened right where I live?"—student G. M.

Conclusion

Science is often touted as being "above" politics, a neutral party in an otherwise agenda-driven, partisan world. Unfortunately, such objectivity does not exist, nor has it ever existed. Rather, it is driven by a combination of social norms and personal ambitions (Graves et al., 2022). Consider the case of Trofim Lysenko (1898–1976), a Soviet scientist who dismissed the widely accepted "Western" view of genetics, and instead championed theories of inheritance that aligned themselves—or rather, were philosophically compatible with—Marxist-Leninist ideology (e.g., only the environment influenced development, and thus plants could be "taught" to survive harsh conditions; Kolchinsky et al., 2017). Had such outlandish theories remained isolated in academic circles, little harm would have been done. However, given Lysenko's fervent adherence to Communist ideals, he quickly became popular with Joseph Stalin, who tasked the scientist with modernizing Soviet agriculture. Unsurprisingly, his promises to greatly increase crop yields and grow citrus in Siberia, among other fantasies, did not come to fruition. Rather, millions of Soviet civilians died of starvation.

This event is but one example of how (pseudo) science can be exploited to serve political, social, and cultural ends. In our own history as Americans, there is perhaps no idea more divisive, more damaging than race being a biologically significant category. However, modern genetics and evolutionary biology strongly reject the notion (Serre & Pääbo, 2004; Graves, 2015; Yudell et al., 2016; Graves & Goodman, 2022). Nevertheless, centuries-old myths regarding the "essential" differences between races persist, leading to continued discrimination and oftentimes violence against non-white Americans. As a biologist, I find the intractability of these ideas maddening and, at times, utterly discouraging. If hundreds of scientists across the globe, across decades, could not extirpate them, who possibly could? As an instructor, however, I know the answer: I can. By shedding light on the complexities of human genetics, it is possible to reduce students' learned racial biases (Donovan et al., 2019, 2020), as well as promote the development of critical scientific literacy (Rodriguez et al., 2022). Discussions of race can and should happen in science classrooms. If we, as instructors, take these opportunities to disentangle biology from race and expose racism for what it truly is—a systemic, sociological issue—we stand a chance of seeing a more equitable future for students (Graves, 2015).

References

Buck v. Bell, 274 U.S. 200 (1927). https://www.loc.gov/item/usrep274200/.

Chou, W-Y. S., Gaysynsky, A., & Vanderpool, R. C. (2022). The COVID-19 misinfodemic: Moving beyond fact-checking. *Health Education & Behavior*, 48(1), 9–13.

Cohen, A. (2017). *Imbeciles: The Supreme Court, eugenics, and the sterilization of Carrie Buck*. Penguin Books, London, UK.

Cooper, R. S. (2005). Race and IQ: Molecular genetics as Deus ex Machina. *American Psychologist*, 60, 71–76.

Darwin, C. (1859). *On the origin of species by means of natural selection, or the preservation of favoured races in the struggle for life*. John Murray, London, UK.

Darwin, C. (1871). *The descent of man: And selection in relation to sex*. John Murray, London, UK.

Davies, G., Tenesa, A., Payton, A., Yang, J., Harris, S. E., Liewald, D., Ke, X., Le Hellard, S., Christoforou, A., Luciano, M., McGhee, K., Lopez, L., Gow, A. J., Corley, J., Redmond, P., Fox, H. C., Haggarty, P., Whalley, L. J., McNeill, G., ... Deary, I. J. (2011). Genome-wide association studies establish that human intelligence is highly heritable and polygenic. *Molecular Psychiatry*, 16(10), 996–1005.

Donovan, B. M., Semmens, R. Keck, P., Brimhall, E., Busch, K. C., Weindling, M., Duncan, A., Stuhlsatz, M., Bracey, Z. B., Bloom, M., Kowalski, S., & Salazar, B. (2019). Toward a more humane genetics education: Learning about the social and quantitative complexities of human genetic variation research could reduce racial bias in adolescent and adult populations. *Science Education, 103*(3), 529–560.

Donovan, B. M., Weindling, M., Salazar, B., Duncan, A., Stuhlsatz, M., & Keck, P. (2020). Genomics literary matters: Support the development of genomics literacy through genetics education could reduce the prevalence of genetic essentialism. *Journal of Research in Science Teaching, 59*(4), 520–550.

Galton, F. (1865). Hereditary talent and character. *Macmillan's Magazine, 12*, 157–166.

Ganna A., Verweij K. J. H, Nivard, M. G., Maier, R., Wedow, R., Busch, A. S., Abdellaoui, A., Guo, S., Sathirapongsasuti, J. F, 23andMe Research Team, Lichtenstein, P., Lundström, S., Långström, N., Auto, A., Harris, K. M., Beecham, G. W., Martin, E. R., Sanders, A. R., Perry, J. R. B., . . . Zietsch, B. P. Large-scale GWAS reveals insights into the genetic architecture of same-sex sexual behavior. (2019). *Science, 365*(6456).

Gibbs, R. W. (1851). Death of Samuel George Morton, MD. *Charleston Medical Journal, 6*, 597.

Gillam, V. (1899, April, 1) The White man's burden (apologies to Rudyard Kipling). [Cartoon] *Judge*.

Golderberger, A. S., & Manksi, C. F. (1995). Review article: The bell curve by Hernstein and Murray. *Journal of Economic Literature, 33*(2), 762–776.

Graves, J. L. (2015). Why the nonexistence of biological races does not mean the nonexistence of racism. *American Behavioral Scientist, 59*(11), 1474–1495.

Graves, J. L., & Goodman, A. H. (2022). *Racism not race: Answers to frequently asked questions*. Columbia University Press.

Graves, J. L., & Johnson, A. (1995). The pseudoscience of psychometry and the bell curve. *The Journal of Negro Education, 64*(3), 277–294.

Graves, J. L., Kearney, M., Barabino, G., & Malcolm, S. (2022). Inequality in science and the case for a new agenda. *PNAS, 119*(10), e2117831119.

Helms, J. E. (1984). Toward a theoretical explanation of the effects of race on counseling: A black and white model. *The Counseling Psychologist, 12*(3), 153–165.

Herstein, R. J., & Murray, C. (1994). *The bell curve: Intelligence and class structure in American life*. Free Press.

Hill, W. D., Davies, N. M., Ritchie, S. J., Skene, N. G., Bryois, J., Bell, S., Di Angelantonio, E., Roberts, D. J., Xueyi, S., Davies, G., Liewald, D. C. M., Porteous, D. J., Hayward, C., Butterworth, A. S., McIntosh, A. M., Gale, C. R., & Deary, I. J. (2019). Genome-wide analysis identifies molecular systems and 149 loci associated with income. *Nature Communications, 10*, 5741.

Hofstra, B., Kulkarni, V. V., Galvez, S. M-N., & McFarland, D. A. (2020). The diversity-innovation paradox in science. *PNAS, 117*(17), 9284–9291.

Hu, B., Shen, N., Li, J. J., Kang, H., Hong, J., Fletcher, J., Greenberg, J., Mailick, M. R., & Lu, Q. (2019). Genome-wide association study reveals sex-specific genetic architecture of facial attractiveness. *PLoS Genetics, 15*(4), e1007973.

Katz, J. H., & Ivey, A. (1977). White awareness: the frontier of racism awareness training. *Personal and Guidance Journal, 55*, 485–487.

Kendi, I. X. (2019). *How to be an antiracist*. One World, London, UK.

Kolchinsky, E. I., Kutschera, U., Hossfeld, U., & Levit, G. S. (2017). Russia's New Lysenkoism. *Current Biology, 27*(19), R1042–R1047.

Li, J. Z., Absher, D. M., Tang, H., Southwick, A. M., Casto, A. M., Ramachandran, S., Cann, H. M., Barsh, G. S., Feldman, M., Cavalli-Sforza, L. L., & Myers, R. M. (2008). Worldwide human relationships inferred from genome-wide patterns of variation. *Science, 319*(5866), 1100–1104.

Linnaeus, C. (1758). *Systema Naturae per regna tria naturae, secundum classes, ordines, genera, species, cum characteribus, differentiis, synonymis, locis*. Editio decima, reformata. Tomus I. Laurentii Salvii, Holmiae, 828 pp.

Lombardo, P. A. (Ed.) (2011). *A century of eugenics: From the Indiana experiment to the human genome era*. Indiana University Press, Bloomington, IN.

Muhammed T. S., & Mathew, S. K. (2022). The disaster of misinformation: A review of research in social media. *International Journal of Data Science and Analytics*, 1–15. Advance online publication.

Okbay, A., Wu, Y., Wang, N., Jayashankar, H., Bennett, M., Nehzati, S. M., Sidorenko, J., Kweon, H., Goldman, G., Gjorgjieva, T., Jiang, Y., Hicks, B., Tian, C., Hinds, D. A., Ahlskog, R., Magnusson, P., Oskarsson, S., Hayward, C., Campbell, A., Porteous, D. J., . . . Young, A. I. (2022). Polygenic prediction of educational attainment within and between families from genome-wide association analyses in 3 million individuals. *Nature Genetics, 54*(4), 437–449.

Plomin, R. & Deary, I. J. (2015). Genetics and intelligence differences: Five special findings. *Molecular Psychiatry, 20*, 98–108.

Randall, D. K. (2019). *Black death at the Golden Gate: The race to save America from the Bubonic Plague*. W. W. Norton & Company.

Rodriguez, A. J., Mark, S., & Nazar, C. R. (2022). Gazing inward in support of critical scientific literacy. *Journal of Science Teacher Education, 33*(2), 125–130.

Rutherford, A. (2020). *How to argue with a racist: What our genes do (and don't) say about human differences*. The Experiment.

Saad, L. (2020). *Me and white supremacy: Combat racism, change the world, and become a good ancestor*. Sourcebooks.

Saini, A. (2019). *Superior: The Return of Race Science*. Beacon Press.

Serre, D., & Pääbo, S. (2004). Evidence for gradients of human genetic diversity within and among continents. *Genome Research, 14*(9), 1679–1685.

Shapiro, D. S. (Director). (2017). *The state of eugenics* [Motion picture]. United States: Brown Doggy Pictures.

Skloot, R. (2010). *The immortal life of Henrietta Lacks*. Crown Publishing.

Southern Poverty Law Center. (2018). *Teaching hard history: American slavery*. Southern Poverty Law Center.

Spencer, H. (1864). *Principles of biology*. William & Norgate.

Sussman, R. W. (2014). *The myth of race: The troubling persistence of an unscientific idea*. Harvard University Press.
Viding, E., & Frith, U. (2006). Genes for susceptibility to violence lurk in the brain. *PNAS, 103*(16), 6085–6086.
Witherspoon, D. J., Wooding, S., Rogers, A. R., Marchani, E. E., Watkins, W. S., Batzer, M. A., & Jorde, L. B. (2007). Genetic similarities within and between human populations. *Genetics, 176*(1), 351–359.
Yudell, M., Roberts, D. R., DeSalle, R., & Tishkoff, S. (2016). Taking race out of human genetics. *Science, 351*(6273), 564–565.

CHAPTER SIX

A Revised Narrative of the Civil Rights Movement and the Power of People in a High School History Course

Elizabeth Veilleux Haynes

> The purpose of education, finally, is to create in a person the ability to look at the world for himself, to make his own decisions, to say to himself this is black or this is white, to decide for himself whether there is a God in heaven or not. To ask questions of the universe, and then learn to live with those questions, is the way he achieves his own identity. But no society is really anxious to have that kind of person around. What societies really, ideally, want is a citizenry which will simply obey the rules of society. If a society succeeds in this, that society is about to perish. The obligation of anyone who thinks of himself as responsible is to examine society and try to change it and to fight it—at no matter what risk. This is the only hope society has. This is the only way societies change.
>
> —James Baldwin, "A Talk to Teachers"

I became a social studies teacher because it felt like a powerful way to empower students to learn about the world around them and learn strategies to be active participants in it. After digging into antiracist pedagogy, it became clear that I could not achieve that goal unless I was prepared to continue learning, unless I was prepared to teach an honest version of history with my students actively present in the narrative. Therefore, in the spring of 2020, I developed an antiracist pedagogical unit that I implemented with my high school history students in 2021. The unit was the final product in a seminar through the Charlotte Teachers Institute (CTI) that explored antiracist pedagogy. In this chapter, I share some of my reflections on the experience of developing the unit and what it was like to teach my unit.

I learned a great deal about my own teaching in the course of creating and facilitating this unit as I examined the instructional practices I was using and what my students were learning. More than that, I also experienced the internal and external struggles that come with learning new ways of teaching. My hope is that these reflections prove a useful tool in your own practice. As I developed my unit, I wrestled with how to keep learning, unlearning, and honesty central to my teaching. I continue to grapple with how to take on the challenges of teaching students today. Students deserve to see themselves reflected in their education and deserve an education that helps them take ownership of the complicated world around them. While this is a challenging task, it is not impossible, and it is our responsibility as educators to face this task head on.

A Total War with Myself

As I sat down to begin developing my unit, I imagined the task would be challenging but not out of reach. After all, I teach American History II, which follows United States history post-Reconstruction to present day. This content could not be more stacked with possibilities to incorporate all that we had been learning about antiracist pedagogy. However, at every turn there were battles to be fought with myself.

The first battle was about where to begin. All teachers know this struggle. If you are reading this book, you have found a place to begin. If I was and am being honest with myself, all of the ways that I teach the curriculum needed reexamining. I needed to allow my students more chances to explore the gains of Black political representation during Reconstruction. I needed to have students analyze the impact of the Great Migration. I needed to make my classroom a less teacher-centered space and let it be driven more by the identities and ideas of my students.

I chose to focus on the civil rights movement because it felt like a place in our curriculum that required urgent reconsideration. Here is *the* unit where we will highlight the Black experience in the United States, and we were expected to cover it in a few class periods? We were supposed to have students learn about the critical events, places, and people involved while leaving out complex and challenging ideas, the collective efforts of activists, the intersectionality of Black experiences, the pain, the joy, and hard work involved in provoking national social, political, and economic change—not to mention the unfinished business? I knew my approach needed to be revised, but I was overwhelmed by all that needed to be reexamined in order to make this unit antiracist. If this sounds like an ambitious task, it was.

Thus, I began battle number two. I was overwhelmed and nervous about doing too much or not doing enough. It would be impossible to teach students everything in the depth that this movement deserves. It would also be a feat to give a true picture of the complexity of this period in US history. This is a continuous struggle in teaching the history of the United States, regardless of the topic, but especially true when the focus is a period that has been so tragically oversimplified.

Ultimately, I decided that people learn best from authentic, meaningful, and relatable stories. This led me to zero in on a few individuals that represent a larger diversity of organizations and strategies. I also considered that the individuals should come from a variety of backgrounds and experiences. It was important to find people who were rooted in the community and provided a window into complexity. I wanted to be very careful when using individuals so that my unit did not perpetuate an unhelpful hero narrative. The hero narrative leaves students with glorified individuals on a pedestal whose achievements are summed up in a few bullet points. These heroes are also often chosen by those creating the dominant narrative to make a point or be an example.

Avoiding the hero narrative has everything to do with how the learning is happening and is not about who you are learning about. Professor Dennis Carlson (2003) of Miami University offers these questions to be used for critical pedagogy of historical heroism:

- How can heroes be formative in shaping how people think about the world and interact with each other? How do heroes reinforce or challenge dominant representations of class, race, gender, sexual, and other identities?
- Where do heroes come from, which is to say, what is their genealogy in various cultural myths and texts?
- How are they circulated, and what interests do they support?
- How has the meaning attached to heroes changed over time and been contested?
- Finally, how can heroic myths be rescripted, subversively re-narrated, and imaginatively reworked in ways that open up democratic possibilities?"

Carlson (2003) argues that education that seeks to move society forward will always need heroes. However, we should be critical of the narrative in order to see more of the story and acknowledge the crucial role of community. A simplistic hero narrative fails to acknowledge the transformative social power of the political ideas of the movement, the vast identities of those involved, and their many forms of antiracist activism (Zamalin, 2019). In order to avoid these pitfalls, I would need to learn a lot more than I already knew.

Reeducation

I started with reeducation. Since my goal was to develop a unit that pushed the boundaries of traditional hero narrative in favor of a fuller understanding of complexity and community, I needed to learn about the diversity I hoped to communicate. I chose to begin by hearing from individuals themselves. It was important to me to heed Alex Zamalin's (2019) advice that turning to people of Color is essential in learning antiracism because they are among those most impacted by the poison of racist ideology.

The same is true when learning a more complete narrative of US history. I realized that I had not had nearly enough exposure to primary sources of the Black scholars, artists, activists, and writers responsible for countless and critical aspects of our nation's story. The fact that I had been able to make it out with a history major and be certified to teach social studies without exposure to the brilliance of myriad Black scholars, artists, activists, and writers is another indication of the structural failures of our education system and the narrow canon of work we allow to define American history. As educators, we bear a responsibility to always be students first. After acknowledging this gap, it was time to get to work. I read, watched, and tried to listen with an open heart and mind.

I started my reeducation with James Baldwin (1963) since it is his quote, from his essay "A Talk to Teachers," that I share at the beginning of each semester of my American History II class:

> I began by saying that one of the paradoxes of education was that precisely at the point when you begin to develop a conscience, you must find yourself at war with your society. It is your responsibility to change society if you think of yourself as an educated person. And on the basis of the evidence—the moral and political evidence—one is compelled to say that this is a backward society. . . . I would try to make him [his student] know that just as American history is longer, larger, more various, more beautiful and more terrible than anything anyone has ever said about it, so is the world larger, more daring, more beautiful and more terrible, but principally larger—and that it belongs to him. (p. 19)

This message from Baldwin to teachers in 1963 remains relevant today and is a must-read for all educators. It is foundational for the kind of urgency required in antiracist pedagogy. Next, I read *The Fire Next Time*, two essays by Baldwin (2013) written in the same year to contextualize the need for the civil rights movement for white Americans. These essays provided personal insight and perspective that showed how racism affected the lives of Black Americans in daily and tangible ways. I made an intentional effort to go beyond traditional mediums of academic learning. By listening to some of the many interviews Baldwin has been a part of over the years, I saw firsthand how he handled active debate with white America. Because of his experiences as a powerful advocate and activist, a writer, a queer person and as someone who lived for a time outside the United States, he was uniquely positioned to show me and my students' perspectives.

Following this, I searched for a deeper understanding of the grassroots, community-focused aspect of the civil rights movement. This was especially evident in the movement that happened on college campuses across the United States, such as the work of the Student Nonviolent Coordinating Committee (SNCC). Ella Baker, a leading organizer in SNCC, expressed the importance of community in an article titled "Bigger than a Hamburger" (Baker, 1960). Baker explained that the civil rights movement is a universal movement and

> this universality of approach was linked with a perceptive recognition that it is "important to keep the movement democratic and to avoid struggles for personal leadership." It was further evident that desire for supportive cooperation from adult leaders and the adult community was also tempered by apprehension that adults might try to "capture" the student movement. The students showed willingness to be met on the basis of equality, but were intolerant of anything that smacked of manipulation or domination. This inclination toward group-centered leadership, rather than toward a leader-centered group pattern of organization, was refreshing indeed to those of the older group who bear the scars of the battle, the frustrations and the disillusionment that come when the prophetic leader turns out to have heavy feet of clay. (p. 8)

Leadership from individuals like Ella Baker, who supported young people in the movement, made it clear that background and age did not disqualify you as an activist or crucial participant. It also made clear the importance of the networks these organizers developed and the mobilization of participants. Being from Virginia and having gone to college in North Carolina, Baker serves as a close to home example for my North Carolina students.

Reading and learning about the life of John Lewis helped guide me in a similar way as did the life of Ella Baker. To better understand John Lewis, I turned to another less conventional source. I read the graphic novel series *March* (Lewis et al., 2013; Lewis et al., 2015; Lewis et al., 2016). This series tells the story of John Lewis's background, how he came to his activism, and major events that happened throughout the movement. Since teaching this unit, I have ordered a class set of the graphic novels for my classroom using a grant provided by my school. I now utilize the novels to establish a timeline of some of the major events and to introduce students to the reality of non-violence as practiced by the Student Nonviolent Coordinating Committee. Since John Lewis had recently passed when I was teaching this unit, his life also provided a different perspective of lifelong political engagement and activism. I watched his TED interview with Bryan Stevenson in order to gain a deeper understanding of Lewis's political legacy and see how Lewis had influenced a new generation of activists like Stevenson.

I turned to Angela Davis to learn about a scholar who is still working in the world today and to start the unlearning process of fear of radical ideas. The life and work of Angela Davis allows a glimpse into how complex identity and a willingness to challenge larger structures at work can lead to a lifetime of advocacy and activism. Also, Davis's life and activism demonstrate the intersection of gender, race, and economic justice. Watching Angela Davis's interview from jail in 1972 (Netflix Film Club, 2020), I began to deconstruct the misunderstanding and fear that surrounds the Black Panther Party and communism. I began to understand the fuller picture of Black activists that the FBI positioned as dangerous and enemies of the state.

Davis extends her activism beyond the borders of the United States to places all over the world. She practices oppositional ideas of antiracism (Zamalin, 2019) and extends the boundaries of liberation. Activists such as Davis participated in and lived out a life of activism that offers a bold reimagining of society while facing the realities of the society in front of them. As Zamalin (2019) writes, "political changes always hinge on theoretical vision. And nothing concerned antiracists more than developing a political theory of freedom and engaged citizenship" (p. 57).

This unit attempted to take a unique perspective on key antiracist leaders of the civil rights movement and embody Zamalin's (2019) notions of antiracist theory. Zamalin teaches us that antiracism is founded in history and grounded in lived experiences of the struggle for racial freedom. In contrast to the focus on individualism and exceptionalism, antiracism is concerned with disruptive collective action, structural change, and urgency. Dismantling racism is not disconnected with addressing other oppressions related to economic, gender, and sexuality. This unit aimed to examine these heroes of the civil rights movement for how they embody these antiracist ideals, effectively dislodging them from the mantle of individual achievement that only perpetuates Western ideology of exceptionalism.

Antiracism work and thus the lessons from the civil rights movement are rooted in the power of the people to self-determination and popular sovereignty. Zamalin's (2019) position is that antiracist sensibility is antiauthoritarian in its argument that the challenges faced by people of Color cannot be solved simply by laws or the power of government but by the collective knowledge of ordinary people. In that same vein, I took what I learned from my own reeducation and incorporated a study of individuals who checked unchecked authority into my unit (Zamalin, 2019). Teaching this notion of the civil rights movement helps provide clarity and connection to the historical period. Antiracism sees legality that is valued over "transformative ethical demands of justice" (Zamalin, 2019, p. 56) as toxic for the collective. This "order over justice" attitude was and has been the view of moderate, white America for too long. The individuals studied in this unit imagined something new and by studying their work, I attempted to show students how to do this structural reimaging for themselves. I was successful in some ways and in most others have so much room to grow. I still have a lot more to learn, but these scholars, activists, and writers were a starting point. I am so grateful to have had the opportunity to learn from them and to introduce my students to them.

Pedagogy

My unit was created for my American History II course at a large suburban high school. South Mecklenburg High School has a diverse student population. The population breakdown of the students, according to the School Diversity Report published by Charlotte Mecklenburg Schools, is 34 percent Hispanic, 24 percent Black, and 34 percent white. I taught this unit in my two traditional American History II classes of sixty-six eleventh and twelfth graders during the spring of 2021. Due to the COVID pandemic, this unit was designed to accommodate teaching students virtually and in person simultaneously. This posed many challenges but also presented exciting opportunities to try new strategies. For example, we utilized the strategies of Jamboard to gather our collective knowledge in pre- and post-reflections and to check in periodically on student learning. Jamboard is a digital bulletin board a teacher can share with students so they can contribute by posting images, asking questions, or making connections and comments. I would post an image of something we had learned about on the previous day and was able to see in a snapshot of sticky notes on the Jamboard what some of the takeaways or remaining questions were. We also utilized breakout Zoom sessions for discussion. This allowed students to interact with one another in a small group setting. However, it was challenging to ensure students were getting the most from these conversations since I was not able to monitor all groups at all times.

The political climate of 2021 was taken into consideration when teaching this unit as well and required careful consideration of how to ensure the classroom was a space where students learned to respectfully ask questions, question others, and listen to new ideas. This continues to be a challenge in a divisive and tense political climate. It was key to begin the year with activities that promoted this environment. I turned to the resources of *Learning for Justice* (formerly Teaching Tolerance) for support. One such resource from *Learning for Justice* (https://www.learningforjustice.org) is the *Civil Rights Done Right: A Tool for Teaching the Movement*, which is a vital tool for any educator wanting to hold themselves accountable.

One of the biggest lessons I learned in teaching this unit was that students took my cue. If I was hesitant and unsure, then students were less willing to buy in. If I modeled genuine curiosity, respect, enthusiasm, and open-mindedness, generally students followed suit. Regardless of whether they drew the same conclusions as one another, students were willing to learn about the new perspectives being presented. This seems like an obvious and universal lesson for teaching, but it was a powerful reminder about how teachers' bias and perspective impact not only what students are learning but how they are learning it.

My students in American History II represent a wide range of identity. I have students from all over the world and all over the United States. My hope for my unit was that my students begin to develop a critical lens through which to see the world. I also hoped that they would see themselves as active participants in the American narrative. My aim was to present all different perspectives, with context, but not commentary and allow students to organically derive relevance for themselves. This is why I used the general guiding questions below to conduct our exploration:

1. What inspired them to their activism?
2. What specific criticism did this person have of American society?
3. What methods/strategies did they use to address these problems?
4. What about this person's work/background makes them a compelling character?
5. What successes/failures did this person achieve/experience?

I began my unit with a pre-assessment conducted through PearDeck. PearDeck is a Google Slides add-on that allows you to embed open-ended questions, drawing tasks, and more. I used this pre-assessment to gauge the previous knowledge my students had about the civil rights movement and to gauge their interests. On the first slide, I had images of a variety of famous civil rights events and asked the students to put a check next to the images they could identify and explain. As student responses came in, we discussed them as a class, and I asked for volunteers to tell what they knew. I followed up by asking students where they had learned about this event and in all cases, with the exception of the March on Washington photo of MLK, they had learned about the event from somewhere other than school. I followed the same procedure for the names of the leaders we would be investigating during our unit, Ella Baker, John Lewis, James Baldwin, Martin Luther King Jr., and Angela Davis. As one might expect all students had heard of Martin Luther King Jr. Generally, a handful of students had heard of the other leaders. In one class however, no one had ever heard of Ella Baker. Finally, I did the same thing with organizations that these leaders represent, SNCC, CORE, SCLC, Black Panther Party, and NAACP. Consistently, students were familiar with the names of the Black Panther Party and the NAACP and unfamiliar with the others.

Then, we moved into a four corners activity, where a statement is put on the board and students decide to agree, strongly agree, disagree, or strongly disagree. This was facilitated by having students write their selection and hold it up to the camera and submit their answer in the Zoom chat box. This activity works more effectively in person and allows for organic discussion about the nature of activism, whose responsibilities social change is, and when action is necessary versus when it is not. Finally, this opening activity concluded with reflection questions intended to get students to think personally about what they want to learn:

1. If your knowledge of the movement is overly simplistic, why do you think that is?
2. What else do you need to know about the civil rights movement?
3. Develop two guiding questions that you can keep coming back to throughout this unit about social change and activism.

I used students' responses to question number two to guide some of the flex time that was built into the unit for student exploration. For example, one student shared that she was interested in a global perspective on the civil rights movement. I found a timeline that laid out a few events happening around the world that provided that global perspective and made it into a Padlet, a digital, interactive map for students to explore (see figure 6.1). I found this opening activity laid a good foundation for students to ask questions, to challenge themselves and me, and to make their learning personal.

74 ~ Elizabeth Veilleux Haynes

Figure 6.1. Screen Shot of Digital Resource—The Winds of Change. Source: Elizabeth Hayes

Each day of the unit was organized to allow time for classroom instruction around the individual who was the focus of the day's discussion. The classroom instruction included sharing the primary sources for each person that guided my learning shared earlier in this chapter. To ensure that students were actively engaging in sources such as a YouTube clip of a James Baldwin's interview on the Dick Cavett Show (2020), I utilized strategies like Think/Pair/Share and three things you learned/two things that surprised/one question you have. These strategies allowed students to process what they were seeing together in a low-stakes way. Students were able to engage honestly and authentically.

To keep track of our learning, I organized the guiding questions into a chart (see figure 6.2) so that students could see the individuals in a larger context, as well as in their own right. I found that as students completed this process, they were able to grasp how individuals fit into their communities and how it takes a multifaceted approach to create social, political, and economic change. These questions allowed students to look not only at the accomplishments of the individuals we were studying but also at their inspirations, experiences, and background. I found that this strategy made our overall analysis throughout the unit cohesive and holistic. However, the drawback of this strategy was the subliminal message that the complex lives of these individuals could be reduced to a row on a chart. I reminded students throughout that this was one way we were capturing our learning

A Revised Narrative of the Civil Rights Movement ⌇ 75

	Their vision of the American Dream	Background of Individual	Organizations that Belonged to/Organized	Issues they Advocated For	Challenges they Faced
Ella Baker					
John Lewis					
James Baldwin					
Martin Luther King Jr.					
Angela Davis					

Figure 6.2. Chart of Guiding Questions. Source: Elizabeth Hayes

but not the only way. As I have continued to teach this unit, I have added more general reflection tools that allow students to make organic and more complete connections.

After four to five days of reflecting on different aspects of the movement from a variety of perspectives, we shifted into making the learning relevant and personal. In this transition from taking the history we were learning and applying it to the world of my students, we had to consider their positionality. From the beginning of the semester in American history, I always have students consider all their experiences and backgrounds. Students do this in the form of an identity map, where they outline things like their religious, geographical, political, and cultural background. They also explore the kinds of work, family, and migration experiences they have had so far in their lives. Reassessing their positionality proved to be an important step to take before students finally considered what the activism of the civil rights movement meant for their personal lives. Students also reflected by coming back to their guiding questions from the pre-assessment and reevaluating what the major takeaways were from the lives and actions of individuals like Baldwin, Davis, Baker, Lewis, King, and Malcolm X.

After seeing this unit in action, one way it falls short is in assuming more background knowledge of students than students had. This will vary depending on where you are teaching and how much students have been exposed to before getting to your class. The unit was built to refresh students' memory of the major events of the civil rights movement and then provide enrichment through the lenses of the individuals we analyzed. In order to build students' knowledge base, it is possible to reorder the individual's past knowledge and supplement with background lessons where there are significant gaps.

Moving to Action

Since the culmination of the unit was to think about their own activism and what they might try to change about the society they are living in, the takeaways were personal. I wanted students to reflect on what they would and can do with their hands, feet, mouths, ears, hearts, and so on. This was an intentional choice because I wanted students reflecting on how this history might inspire them. We started this process with a whole class reflection on the social issues being addressed by the civil rights movement in which students highlighted issues such as integration, quality education, issues of poverty, and criticism of military actions (the war in Vietnam). Students then reflected on social issues facing our world today. Students highlighted the COVID pandemic, police brutality, anti-immigrant attitudes, environmental issues, quality education, and access to health care.

After this whole class reflection, students decided on three issues they felt were the most pressing. Once students decided on the top three issues for them, they were asked to identify specific strategies and actionable steps they could take to address their issues of focus. Students were given an outline of a person to brainstorm what they would do with their hands (tangible action), what they would do with their feet (where they might need to go), what they would need to do with their mouths (what they needed to say), what they would need to do with their minds (what thoughts/problem-solving skills/mindsets they needed to have), what they would need to do with their heart (what feelings they might have) while they take the actions. After the first draft was created, students narrowed their focus and created a final draft either digitally or on paper. Students wrote a one- to two-page reflection to explain their thinking during this process and to make evidence-based connections to the aspects of the movement that we had studied.

Mishaps and Reflections

Antiracist pedagogy stresses the importance of challenging systems of racism. I wanted action to be a vital part of this unit. Simply learning about racism and antiracism is not enough. The projects described above were our attempt to develop concrete strategies we could use to deploy antiracist activism. However, there were some unintended consequences of these pedagogies. The move to the action portion of the unit had the unintended consequence of making it feel like the challenges of our world today were all the student's burden to bear. This culmination did not do enough to allow students to use their unique talents and passions. Going forward, I would like the culmination to highlight students' joy.

Another aspect of this was in my identity as a white, female educator, along with the largest majority of teachers in the United States. I did not do enough to name the ways my identity informs how I see the world in order to model that for my students. I am often reminded how it is essential for me to model the open reflection on my personal perspectives in regard to race. I realized I was not open enough with students about my own self-reflection and positionality throughout this unit. I cannot ask my students to be vulnerable and honest if I am not doing the same. I have to model naming my experiences as a white woman in the United States in order to have students feel comfortable to do the same. Because of students' varied experiences in spaces where race is being discussed, I need to make it clear what the expectations are in this space. This is primarily so that students know that they do not have to hold back.

Going forward, I would like to change the culmination of the unit to be about both individual impact and systemic change. I would focus more on what the students' larger lessons were and how those lessons might impact their perspectives, attitudes and actions. The objective of the unit is for students to walk away with an assured confidence in their ability to be critical participants in the world around them.

Reflective Practice

One of the biggest lessons that I learned throughout the teaching of this unit was how important a willingness to let go of fear was for me as the teacher. A lot of my anxiety throughout teaching this unit concerned deconstructing what I was actually afraid of, unlearning my associations of "bad" words and realizing that my whole job is about presenting the good, the bad, and the ugly. I am not telling anyone how to think, but I am teaching students to approach all things with a critical lens and to be thoughtful participants in their society. My goal was and is to follow what James Baldwin says we should do in order to have a free society. Baldwin (1963) reminds us we should "ask questions of the universe, and then learn to live with those questions" (p. 678) in order to achieve our own identities.

The other big lesson was that my own personal learning will never and should never be done. I should always be considering what I will incorporate next, whose stories are being left out, and ways in which I have not told the whole story. One of the most wonderful things about being a teacher is that you are a lifelong student. If I am not challenging my assumptions about what I know, I will fail my students. This can feel like a daunting task but my strategy is to learn one new thing each time I teach something, try one new resource every couple of months, listen to one new podcast, or watch one new documentary from a new perspective. This has had the effect of not only causing me to be able to present and incorporate new ideas into my curriculum but it has also kept me excited about the material. I am able to pass this excitement along to my students.

Moving Forward

My practice continues to evolve every day, and since implementing this unit, I have expanded my thinking about how and what to teach about the civil rights movement. I have also developed a civil rights timeline that involves a public display element. This continues to grow and change as I figure out ways to incorporate strength, resilience, and culture, rather than just political events. I am continuing to attempt to expand their perspectives by showing documentaries such as *King in the Wilderness* (Films Media Group, 2018), *I Am Not Your Negro* (Peck et al., 2017) and the *Summer of Soul* (Questlove, 2021). Each of these emphasizes the humanity of the experience of Black Americans. I have also created an extension that connects other movements to the global civil rights movement and the other social movements within the United States including the Farm Workers Movement, Women's Liberation, the American Indian Movement. Without this piece, students were not seeing that one group's actions and decisions always impact others.

Social studies teachers receive a lot of criticism from politicians, state and local education officials, social media and the media generally. Schools are always reflections of the social, cultural, and political debates of the larger society. Therefore, it is to be expected that there would be arguments over the space where students are supposed to be learning about the history of our nation and other nations. Our students deserve a better education and our work requires examination. In his introduction to *Ratchetdemic: Reimaging Academic Success*, Chris Edmin (2021) writes, "Being ratchetdemic is allowing our swords . . . to bring the culture of young people to the fore and allow them to leverage their natural genius to overcome the oppression" (p. 10). Allowing students to leverage their natural genius means telling students honestly about the history of our nation and giving them space in school to actively explore their place in the narrative. Moving toward honest history doesn't mean that teachers were necessarily being actively dishonest with history in the past, although that has been the case in many instances. Honest history requires that we actively expand the narrative and give students tools to understand and overcome oppression they see in our society.

References

Baker, E. (1960). Bigger than a hamburger. *Southern Patriot, 18*(5), 4.
Baldwin, J. (2008). A talk to teachers (1963). *The Yearbook of the National Society for the Study of Education, 107*(2), 15–20. https://doi.org/10.1111/j.1744-7984.2008.00154.x.
Baldwin, J. (2013). *The fire next time*. Vintage.
Carlson, D. (2003). Troubling heroes: Of Rosa Parks, multicultural education, and critical pedagogy. *Cultural Studies ↔ Critical Methodologies, 3*(1), 44–61. https://doi.org/10.1177/1532708603239267.
Edmin, C. (2021). *Ratchetdemic: Reimagining academic success*. Beacon Press.
Films Media Group (2018). *King in the wilderness. Films on demand*. Retrieved June 22, 2022, from https://fod.infobase.com/PortalPlaylists.aspx?wID=149262&xtid=148962.
Lewis, J., Aydin, A., & Powell, N. (2013). *March: Book one*. Top Shelf Productions.
Lewis, J., Aydin, A., Powell, N., & Ross, C. (2015). *March: Book two*. Top Shelf Productions.
Lewis, J., Aydin, A., Powell, N., & Walton, L. (2016). *March: Book three*. Top Shelf Productions.
Netflix Film Club (2020, July 14). 13th | Dr. Angela Davis puts the system on trial [Video]. YouTube. https://www.youtube.com/watch?v=tfCupHW8W44.
Peck, R., Grellety, R., Peck, H., Strauss, A., Adebonojo, H., Ross, B., Ross, T., Aïgi, A., Jackson, S. L., Belafonte, H., Brando, M., Cavett, D., Bush, G. W., Baldwin, J., & Bush, G. W. (2017). *I am not your negro*. Kino Lorber.
Questlove. (2021). The summer of love (. . . or, when the revolution could not be televised). Retrieved June 22, 2022, from https://www.imdb.com/title/tt11422728/.
The Dick Cavett Show. (2020, June 24). James Baldwin discusses racism [Video]. YouTube. https://www.youtube.com/watch?v=WWwOi17WHpE.
Zamalin, A. (2019). *Antiracism: An introduction*. New York University Press.

CHAPTER SEVEN

Middle School Science Students Learn How Structural Racism in the US Shaped Our COVID Experience

Evie Elson

> The very structured way in which a disaster is experienced, forces us to—at least at the moral and ethical level——to really pay attention . . . to the differentiated way in which harm is experienced. And if we don't, then we end up actually becoming part of the problem.
>
> —Eddie Glaude

The day before school shut down in Charlotte, North Carolina, on March 13, 2020, I had just finished teaching my eighth-grade biology students about the difference between an epidemic and a pandemic. They learned that, unlike an epidemic (when a disease outbreak occurs in *one* location), a pandemic is when a disease outbreak spreads *worldwide*. When school shut down, my students could determine that COVID had developed into a pandemic. What they likely could *not* determine at that time, however, was the effect this pandemic would have on our lives. As the coronavirus swept through the country, its impact shed light on patterns in our society that, although shocking to some, are not new. The virus revealed the ugly inequities in our economy, job market, our health care system, and our access to basic resources. The inequities did not reveal themselves in light of a crisis, however. In fact, these patterns are ingrained in the foundations of our country, causing disproportionate harm and destruction to communities of Color. This pandemic was considered "unprecedented," yet its effects are not unprecedented. They are expected (Elson, 2020).

It was with this understanding of the permanence and pervasiveness of racism that I developed my antiracist pedagogical unit on microbes and disease. First, we defined types of microbes and the disease outbreaks that could result from certain pathogens. Then, we analyzed how structural racism in the United States shaped our COVID experience. This unit later transpired into a second part on biotechnology's development. Over the course of the unit, students were able to refine their understanding of biology and critically think about the ways in which science is impacted by society and vice versa. But before any of this could take place—before I began any of the lessons—a more essential development had to take place: my self-reflection as a white teacher. In this chapter, I will describe the development of my antiracist pedagogical unit, beginning with that crucial component.

Critical Reflection: My Takeaways

> When someone with the authority of a teacher, say, describes the world and you are not in it, there is a moment of psychic disequilibrium, as if you looked in the mirror and saw nothing.
>
> —Adrienne Rich

In the above quote, Adrienne Rich describes the power a teacher can hold in a classroom. To that end, teachers must dig deep and take risks in spite of this responsibility. To engage in antiracist pedagogy is to make oneself vulnerable to making mistakes. Sometimes these mistakes will make themselves known immediately, and sometimes it will take months, even years, to notice the ways in which your reasoning, methodology, or approach is ineffective or flawed. I believe that to be a truly antiracist educator is to lean into your evolution as a teacher, but more importantly, as a person. I begin this section by sharing two of my biggest takeaways from building and rebuilding, teaching, and reteaching my unit.

Firstly, teaching this unit showed me how learning from our students is an integral part of antiracist teaching. The teacher is not the gatekeeper of knowledge. Especially as a white woman teaching students of Color, paying attention to my positionality was crucial. Discussing issues of race and class required me to position myself as a facilitator, not a specialist or the primary holder of knowledge. By explicitly calling out the fact that, as a white person in America, I am afforded different opportunities and access to resources, I was better able to engage in authentic conversations. Not only did this help to develop a level of trust with my students of Color and allow them to drive the conversation with openness and honesty, but it also provided a good model for the few white students I teach to approach these conversations from a place of empowerment and engagement, and not defensiveness. Overall, the teacher-as-facilitator dynamic enables everyone to be an equal contributor with valuable knowledge and ideas to offer.

Secondly, I recognized the variability of a curriculum, depending on the context in which I am teaching. Especially since this unit revolves around COVID, an unpredictable and constantly mutating virus, its effects on our world are also variable. When designing any curriculum, but especially antiracist curriculum that relies on critical analysis of our past and our present, the ability for the curriculum to breathe and evolve as our world does, it is of utmost importance. The beauty of antiracist pedagogy is that it is a tool for which teachers can hold themselves accountable to considering themselves, and the content they teach, as works in progress.

My Learning

In the summer of 2020, when I was first designing my curriculum unit, the notion of abolitionist teaching, a term coined by the academic, writer, and activist Bettina Love, took on greater meaning. The murders of Breonna Taylor, George Floyd, Ahmaud Arbery, Rayshard Brooks, Tony McDade—and too many others—sparked a gross reckoning and reimagining of our country's deeply entrenched racist systems among educators. Then, all of the sudden, schools closed. Many teachers like myself took the opportunity to pause and reflect on the way our own classrooms were perpetuating ignorance to our country's history and its legacy of racial oppression. As I was preparing to facilitate an antiracist curriculum, I had to learn things that I didn't already know. I would even consider it a process of *unlearning*. As a result of my (mis)education, in which the dominant narrative centers whiteness both in primary and secondary education and in our teacher-training programs, the act of my unlearning felt like an act of resistance to that narrative.

To begin my unlearning, I started with reading. A colleague of mine recommended Christopher Emdin's (2016) *For White People Who Teach in the Hood . . . And Rest of Y'all Too* to a group of beginner teachers. I teach at a Title I school in which more than 90 percent of students are students of Color, and the majority are eligible for free and reduced lunch. Learning to teach students whose education thus far had largely erased their experiences meant having to turn what I believed to be true about teacher-student relationships upside down. I was not in a position of authority simply because I was the teacher. I had to earn trust and respect from my students, by centering their experiences over mine. Emdin wrote, "The work for white folks who teach in urban schools, then, is to unpack their privileges and excavate the institutional, societal, and personal histories they bring with them when they come to the hood" (Emdin, 2016, p. 15). For me, this is a process that never ends.

To prepare to teach this unit specifically—virtually in 2021, and in-person in the 2022 academic school year—I attended online webinars, listened to podcasts, and read articles that addressed the ways in which institutionalized racism in America impacts one's experience with the virus based on their identity. During the first year of the pandemic, scholars such as Eddie Glaude, Deena Simmons, Bettina Love, Ghouldy Muhammed, Ibram X. Kendi, and Kimberle Crenshaw committed to ensuring that discussions about COVID's impact on America focused on a deeper analysis of how America's racial history continues to shape the experiences of people of Color today.

As I researched, I paid close attention to how the intersectionality of one's identity dictated their risk of exposure to the virus. In order to communicate these nuances, my unit would need to address the amalgamation of issues concerning employment, access to health care, the criminal justice system, xenophobia, and immigration. For example, the COVID crisis revealed the racist implications of US immigration policy, as responses to cases arising at the Mexico-US border went largely unacknowledged. Instead of distributing funds to supply public health resources at the borders, funds were instead steered toward converting buildings into "quarantine facilities," which simply confined large groups of people to designated buildings (SPLC, 2020). Those detained at the border were thus rendered vulnerable to the spread of the virus due to the lack of social distance the detention centers afforded them. Some immigrants seeking asylum were refused upon arrival, due to a proclamation prohibiting certain immigrants from entering the United States. While the Trump administration claimed this was to preserve employment opportunities for current US citizens, the targeting of immigrants coming from the southern border suggests this decision had a more racialized and sinister objective (Loweree et al., 2020).

Similarly, jails and prisons allow for little to no social distancing. The pandemic has brought to light injustice associated specifically with jails, where people who have yet to pay bail, are forced to stay. Inability to pay bail is the most common reason jail populations are so large, putting those who either work or are incarcerated there, at risk of getting sick (The Marshall Project, 2020). The Marshall Project (2020) collected data from prisons around the country to expose the extent to which imprisoned people were denied the right to receive adequate health care to protect them from exposure to the virus.

Acknowledging the trauma associated with these discussions, I needed to think of a way to maintain the integrity of what it means to engage in antiracist pedagogy. That is, ensuring that my students could refer to their own lived experiences in ways that are empowering and not distressing. Bettina Love encapsulated this idea when discussing abolitionist teaching with the *Education Liberation Network*: "What we can do is make sure we don't teach just the trauma; that we teach the pain, the love, the joy, the resistance, equally, and tell our full story of our humanity. That's what makes us human—is when we tell our full story" (Love, 2019).

With this in mind, I wanted my students to know their experiences are valuable. So, when tackling issues of race and inequality, I ensured they could use their own realities as reference points. I wanted them to be able to put their experiences into words to advocate for themselves and others. Therefore, the lessons throughout the unit offered choice boards that allowed students to pick and choose their approach to a certain assignment. Choice boards are a pedagogical tool that provide students with different courses of action to reach the same objective. For example, the objective for one lesson was to research and analyze how COVID impacted a community (beyond health measures) based on their intersectional identities. A student could choose to research Asian American communities, immigrant communities, incarcerated populations, or a population of their choice. Students not only had several options for the communities they wanted to research, but they also had a list of ways to engage with that research. They could watch videos, listen to podcasts, read articles, observe art, or engage with interactive websites. Choice boards also offered flexibility and creativity when it came to the end-of-unit project, described below.

Designing Pedagogy

While antiracist teaching is not new, the political climate in 2020 provided space and impetus for educators to reconsider their content and ways in which they were teaching it. Pioneered by Bettina Love and other activities and educators in 2020, Abolitionist Teaching encapsulates a method of teaching that acknowledges the deeply entrenched inequities in our education system and recognizes the need to dismantle the system and reimagine the way we teach children.

Antiracist teaching demands a descriptive, rather than prescriptive pedagogy, that allows both teachers and students to collaborate and explore together. In the winter of 2021 and 2022, I had the privilege of working with other eighth-grade science teachers, who helped me shape the unit to meet the needs of our students after transitioning back to in-person learning. Collaborative work became a crucial component of this unit as we supported each other in leaning into challenging conversations with students.

As I designed this curriculum, I wanted to ensure that students would have a wide range of ways to engage with the material. Once the students had rooted themselves in the foundational understanding of microbes and how they worked, we could move into deeper discussions of how organisms, too small to be seen by the naked eye, could wreak such havoc on us—namely, in the form of disease outbreaks. With COVID still dictating our lives, the unit was not only relevant but also deeply personal.

After learning about microbes and the pathogens that can harm us, we addressed the broader social implications of outbreaks such as COVID. The unit thus began with an inquiry-based lesson that required students to analyze COVID Racial Data tracker (https://covidtracking.com/race), a collection of data collected by Ibram X. Kendi and his research team on COVID's impact on America according to race. Next, I presented students with a Thinglink (https://www.thinglink.com)—an interactive web application—that included resources to explore a topic of their choice. Their task was to identify the ways in which COVID had impacted certain populations *beyond* just health measures. How has COVID impacted the way we make policy? The way we interact with each other? The way our vulnerable populations live and work? The Thinglink topics included immigrant populations, incarcerated populations, Asian American populations and essential workers.

The unit then transpired in various ways, from individual research, to grade-level discussions about the misconceptions surrounding COVID and its sociopolitical effects in our school's Verizon Innovation Lab, to research projects that enabled students to creatively showcase their knowledge in the form of comic strips, movies, posters, and stories.

Action: Students Respond to Racial Injustice through Project-Based Work

> At first it was horrible until [the co-teacher] and Ms. Elson broke it all down to us that everyone was having misconceptions about race with Covid, Race doesn't matter with covid-19 its comes in many ways and nobody like to wear mask.... Covid is nothing to play with.
>
> —Janiya, eighth-grade student

When I asked a group of my students to explore the COVID Racial Data Tracker website and report on what they noticed or wondered about the data, I was met with skepticism and resentment. What I had considered to be clear—that the data was pointing at a larger systemic American problem—my students considered to be a blatant attack on the individual behaviors of people of Color. When I posed the question "Why do you think COVID is impacting people of Color more than white people?" my students saw this as a question hinting at blame on these communities—that they don't wear masks, or they socialize too much, or do not care about getting sick. It was a major oversight on my part. I had not even considered the fact that providing context—namely, that America's historic systems of oppression impacts the way disease is experienced in America due to the inequities in our healthcare system, in jobs, and in housing—would have been so crucial to pursuing these difficult discussions in a responsible way. I had to pause, reflect, and return to the discussion when emotions had settled the following day.

Needless to say, the unit was not "one size fits all"—in fact, the structure of my lessons changed across my classes. For some, I had to apologize and retroactively highlight the larger structural issues at play. I told my students that I had neglected to preface our lesson with a discussion about America's historic failure to protect all Americans from harm, regardless of race or class. Without the context, the data presented could have been interpreted as a suggestion that COVID rates among people of Color was a result of individual behaviors. My transparency in admitting this oversight opened up more honest conversations about race and class and rebuilt the trust that I feared I had broken. For other classes, I was able to preemptively modify my lessons to have that discussion before diving into the data.

Once this groundwork was established, we were able to move on to look into more underlying social issues. I asked the students to choose a research topic about how different groups may have experienced COVID in nuanced ways, beyond health measures. I asked students to research populations such as essential workers, immigrants, Asian Americans, and incarcerated populations, and then come up with ideas about how the government or individuals could respond to the issues they found. For example, I encouraged them to ask questions like: How could we speak out against hate crimes toward Asian Americans as a result of xenophobic narratives perpetuated in the media? How could the government better protect incarcerated people who were unable to socially distance themselves in prisons? How did the government's receipt of the immigrant population change based on ethnicity and race during COVID?

By the end of the unit, I asked a few students to reflect on what they learned, and how their science class had engaged in discussions of race. Chassidy, one of the students who expressed offense to the lesson at first, came to an evolved conclusion: "[Our science class] showed that some races are impacted more than another simply due to the fact that they [people of Color] are less protected. . . . That some were very unprepared and that the government protect others more than others. Due to living conditions . . . I would put more money into healthcare and schooling so they are more prepared for a pandemic like this. Also, in housing to make sure they are affordable."

Following the class discussions, I then had students consider a real-life scenario in which they had to advocate for various communities in the event that another pandemic arose. My classroom therefore became a mock city council meeting room, whereby community groups including restaurant owners, grocery store clerks, landlords, teachers, parents, health care workers and farmers testified before the mayor and their city council of Charlotte, North Carolina. Their testimonies encouraged their representatives to consider their unique experiences with COVID-19 and how their local government could have done more to protect them. Students applied financial literacy skills in discussing Charlotte's city budget, critiqued its current spending, and suggested a new budget proposal in the event of this new pandemic "COVID-22."

In summary, the unit unfolded in a way that can best be summarized as a valuation of descriptive, as opposed to prescriptive, pedagogical methods. The flexible methodology allowed for difficult, yet authentic conversations to flourish, providing a space in which teachers and students were equals. As a final project, my co-teacher and I decided to combine this unit on disease outbreaks with the succeeding unit on biotechnology. We asked students to create a story, movie trailer, or comic on a topic of their choice—COVID, cloning, or GMOs. Our students were excited to showcase their creativity and content knowledge on their own terms, as opposed to on the terms of a standardized assessment.

In table 7.1, I highlight some of the student responses to the key questions in lesson 2 in our unit: COVID in America. In textbox 7.1, I share the guidelines I created for a mock city council meeting in lesson 5 of the unit and textbox 7.2 are some of the student responses to those mock city council meeting guidelines. As a final example of some of the work students produced, figure 7.4a shows a comic titled "Batman v. Joker: Science Edition," which conflates the idea of a villain-hero dynamic with the virus and a vaccine, and transposes the concept into the classic DC comic story. Figure 7.4b depicts an excerpt from a personalized story that documents the state of society, politics, and healthcare during COVID. Figure 7.4c is a hand drawn comic depicting life at home during the quarantine period of the pandemic.

Table 7.1. Student Responses to Key Questions about COVID in America. Source: Evie Elson

Daneida: COVID in America

Your topic:	How has COVID impacted this community?	What is the government's role in protecting this community?	What is YOUR role in helping this community?
Impact on Asian American communities	It has affected them negatively, because Anti-Asian attacks and harassment have risen significantly ever since the Covid-19 pandemic started	The US has had a long history of racism. What they should do is pass some laws in order to protect Asians from this harassment or start an organization that will be run by Asians to help Asians financially.	The most simple thing ever, just treat them as human beings. Nothing about them should be stereotyped when you don't even know the person, it's rude to assume stuff, so just treat them with respect.

Na'Kiem: COVID in America

Your topic:	How has COVID impacted this community?	What is the government's role in protecting this community?	What is YOUR role in helping this community?
Impact on essential workers	Covid impacted this community in a negative way and unfair way because most essential workers are still working outside everyday while most of other jobs can work at home.	The government's role in protecting this community is that they could provide more safety equipment or moderate the workers and make sure they aren't sick and in good conditions	My role in this is an supporting role because i support and some days on weekends i help my father with truck driving and moving equipment

JP: COVID in America

Your topic:	How has COVID impacted this community?	What is the government's role in protecting this community?	What is YOUR role in helping this community?
Impact on incarcerated people	They are forced to stay in a building where there are a lot of people living in the same cell and small areas so people get infected easily.	Make more space for inmates or give house sentences, and also give everyone ppe.	Staying inside the home

Lin: COVID in America

Your topic:	How has COVID impacted this community?	What is the government's role in protecting this community?	What is YOUR role in helping this community?
Immigrant families	Covid impacted families don't have health insurance. They are having to leave the country and leave their loved ones and their friends	To give immigrant families the same rights and health care	To help them with their health I think and need health insurance to be able to be in good health

Textbox 7.1. Guidelines for a Mock City Council Meeting from Lesson 5

Charlotte City 2022 Budget is $2.7 Billion. Pretend there is a new COVID-22 virus . . . what issues should be prioritized in this budget? What concerns should the City Council consider?

City Council/Mayor—You are the group of elected officials who listen to the community groups. You need to decide on how the COVID budget should be distributed and what kind of things you want to prioritize in preparation for another virus.

Community Groups—Your role is to tell the City Council what to prioritize for their budget. Remember: City Council works for you. For your government to effectively do its job, it needs to hear about what you are passionate about because you bring a unique set of experiences to the table and deserve to have a voice. This is democracy, and public engagement ensures its success.

TV reporters—You are a reporter for WBTV News in Charlotte, North Carolina. You have been assigned to cover the City Council meeting. Most importantly, you need to report on the debate over how to prepare for COVID-22. You will be asked to give a "live report" by filming parts of the meeting or taking notes by asking the community groups questions.

Textbox 7.2. Student Responses to Mock City Council from Lesson 5

Sonia:
This first pandemic affected local restaurant owners by people no longer not wanted to go out, profits were declining, everything had to be rearranged. Yes, I did struggle to pay my staff because my profits were declining because of the fact that much people didn't want to come eat at restaurants. I want the city council to provide money for us local restaurants so we can be able to provide for our family and our self's, and more resources to keep people safe and myself so I don't get my family sick and provide them food, their needs basically.

Arnaldo:
As a cashier at food lion there are many things that put our safety at risk. There are hundreds of people that shop here every day and some of them do a good job with wearing masks but there are people who refuse to wear masks. The only PPE (personal protective equipment) we have are cleaning wipes, hand sanitizer, masks. If we want to stay safe we should be provided with more PPE. Security should be added because they would give people masks when entering the store. If people still refuse to wear a mask they should be kicked out and cannot return until they wear a mask. Hand sanitizer should also be put around the store to stay sanitary.

Scarlett:
Hello. I am a concerned parent who is stuck in between two options for my children's education. In my opinion, I suggest that you should raise everyone's budget around the world to about $2.1 million for safe sanitary things, so we could help prevent this pandemic . . . I'm in the process of making a decision between sending my kids to school and having them socialize to others, or keeping my children at home while they're learning virtually . . . IF they learn virtually, nobody to watch my kids while I'm at work. I do feel safe sending my children to school but, it would also be super risky. Please hear out and respond to my testimony. It would be very much needed. Thank you.

Figure 7.4a. "Batman vs. Joker, Science Edition" by Anthony and Donnie. Source: Evie Elson

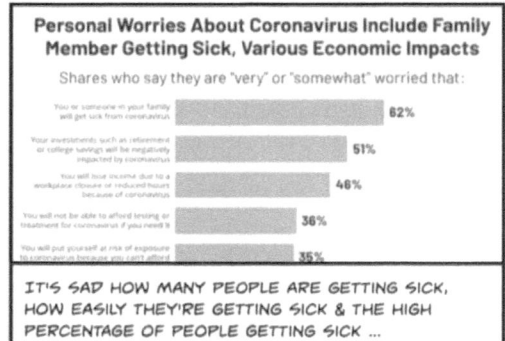

Figure 7.4b. "COVID-19" by Ashley. Source: Evie Elson

Figure 7.4c. My One Question" by Damion. Source: Evie Elson

Conclusion

Antiracist and abolitionist teaching is liberation. For both the students and the teacher, it frees us from the constructs that limit our creativity and our capacity to reimagine the classroom space. While many teachers, including myself, lament the restrictions of state standards and assessments that loom over our heads, we have the opportunity to expand our understanding of what it means to be standards-aligned. Being an antiracist teacher does not mean you have to squeeze a discussion about race or racism into an unrelated lesson.

If anything, forcing those discussions into unrelated topics would be insincere. A science lesson on fossils could be about just that, but it could be taught in a way that is antiracist. In other words, antiracist pedagogy is a *way* of teaching, it is not necessarily content-based. No matter the subject, age level, or demographic—to encourage openness and critical thinking, to have students depend on their own experiences and identities to make sense of concepts, to position oneself as a learner in the classroom alongside your students, is to foster an abolitionist agenda.

Throughout the unit on COVID, my students were able to process what was certainly a traumatic period of their lives—a period that is still ongoing, and whose impact will be apparent for years. They could unpack their own experiences and empathize with others whose experiences may have been different. Part of that process was coming to terms with their own identities, and me coming to terms with mine. In this way, I was both a teacher and a student, which made the experience all the more authentic and fulfilling. By the end of the unit, as a group we had envisioned a future in which disease and its destruction could be curbed—a future in which those in positions of power would listen to their communities, understand their unique experiences and circumstances, and work to protect them.

While I hope for a future world in which the rigidity of our current education systems loosens to reflect the more dynamic and innovative society we live in today, for now, I hope to continue to be part of those communities of educators who can challenge each other to think outside the box, to "unpack their privileges and excavate the institutional, societal, and personal histories they bring" (Emdin, 2016, p. 15). Only then can we commit to antiracist pedagogy that is honest and true.

References

Benjamin, R. (2013). *People's science: Bodies and rights on the stem cell frontier*. Stanford University Press.

Crenshaw, K. (n.d.). *Under the blacklight: The intersectional vulnerabilities that COVID lays bare*. Retrieved March 30, 2020, from https://open.spotify.com/episode/77uJB Bf0L9d1CRQN1YB37d?si=UUrtbqJ2Rr2uKgV-IsxPjA.

Elson, E. (2020). Lessons to learn from COVID-19: How our students can reflect on the pandemic's exposure of America's racial inequities in order to envision a better future. *Journal of Curriculum and Pedagogy, 17*(2), 228–231.

Emdin, C. (2016). *For white folks who teach in the hood . . . and the rest of y'all too: Reality pedagogy and urban education*. Beacon Press.

Love, B. L. (2019). *We want to do more than survive: Abolitionist teaching and the pursuit of educational freedom*. Beacon Press.

Loweree, Jorge, Reichlin-Melnick, A., & Ewing, W. (2020, May 27). "The impact of COVID-19 on noncitizens and across the US immigration system." American Immigration, https://www.americanimmigrationcouncil.org/research/impact-covid-19-us-immigration-system.

The Marshall Project (2020, September 23). "A state-by-state look at coronavirus in prisons," https://www.themarshallproject.org/2020/05/01/a-state-by-state-look-at-coronavirus-in-prisons.

Repurposing Our Pedagogies: Abolitionist Teaching. (2020, July 12). https://www.youtube.com/watch?v=9azT7_AyDQ4&list=PLsrLXy6i4sTrbng4-tCDWDXshX1sYAapG.

Prison Policy Initiative. (2020, September 11). Responses to the COVID-19 pandemic." https://www.prisonpolicy.org/virus/virusresponse.html.

SPLC (2020). Trump's racist response to COVID-19 endangers all Americans, including immigrants.

Necessary Damage

A Conclusion

Angela V. Walker and Erin T. Miller

> The time will always come when teachers must ask themselves if they will follow the mold or blaze a new trail. There are serious risks that come with this decision. It essentially boils down to whether one chooses to do damage to the system or to the student.
>
> —Christopher Edmin

In the preceding chapters, we have shown how antiracist pedagogy is a necessary approach for addressing the inequities that persist in education due to racist mindsets, policies, practices, and structures. We hope the snapshots of the curriculum described in this book underscore the idea that antiracist pedagogy is messy yet necessary, if education is going to be relevant to all students in the classroom. The purpose of these concluding remarks is to emphasize the key takeaways that reinforce this idea that can be found in each of the preceding chapters.

First, antiracist pedagogy intentionally utilizes resources that promote diversity and equity. Representation matters. Students are empowered by characters that look like them, stories that draw on their values, and images that portray them in a positive light. When implementing these resources, educators must be sensitive to ensure they do not limit their examples to those associated with trauma; students need also to explore the joy of their history and heritage.

Second, the teacher's process of unlearning is equally as important as what the student learns. Antiracist teaching calls upon educators to reject white supremacist assumptions, systems, and policies and to relearn fuller, more equitable picture of what it means to both learn and to teach. In doing so, teachers learn how to reconfigure practices and systems that consider the perspectives of those who have been historically marginalized and silenced.

Third, antiracist pedagogy does not fit neatly into a prescriptive paradigm, and it requires the continual reflection, evaluation, and adaptation of the educators who employ it. Because it is a continual process of becoming attuned to the ways that racism and white supremacy manifest in our lived realities, antiracist pedagogy is by no means perfect. Fourth, despite the attempts to delegitimize and stigmatize antiracist pedagogy as propaganda, antiracist pedagogy maintains a significant role in democratic education. It aims to inspire students to take action toward fulfilling the promise of American democracy. Fulfilling the promise of American democracy and for the students who comprise that democracy means, as Edmin (2016) reminds us in the opening quote to this conclusion, doing damage to systems that have failed them in order to build better systems that do not just serve, but save, us all.

References

Emdin, C. (2016). *For white folks who teach in the hood . . . and the rest of y'all too: Reality pedagogy and urban education.* Beacon Press.

About the Authors

Editors

Erin T. Miller (she/her/hers) is an associate professor at the University of North Carolina at Charlotte (UNCC). She is a former first- and second-grade teacher. She codeveloped and currently directs the Antiracist Graduate Certificate Program at UNCC. Her scholarship examines the intersection of racial identity, childhood socialization, and teacher education.

Angela V. Walker (she/her/hers) is an English teacher at West Charlotte High School and an adjunct lecturer in the Antiracist Graduate Certificate Program at UNCC. She is deeply committed to practical deployments of antiracist pedagogy and has conducted numerous workshops exploring the intersection of faith-based epistemologies, education, and antiracism.

Contributors

Pablo Chialvo (he/him/his) is a lecturer in the biology department at Appalachian State University, where he primarily teaches large introductory courses for non-majors. He is an active contributor to numerous diversity, equity, and inclusion (DEI) initiatives at the university, including allyship programs and curriculum development groups.

Evie Elson (she/her) served as an eighth-grade science teacher and the Social Emotional Learning curriculum lead at Whitewater Middle School in Charlotte, North Carolina. Elson became a Teach for America corps member after earning her BA in political science from Princeton University in 2019. In 2020, Elson published an article titled "Lessons to Learn from COVID-19: How Our Students Can Reflect on the Pandemic's Exposure of America's Racial Inequities in Order to Envision a Better Future" in the *Journal of Curriculum and Pedagogy*. Elson is dedicated to reforming the education system from the inside out—ensuring that classrooms are spaces of empowerment and activism. This fall she will be moving to California to continue her career in education.

Anne Galligan (she/her/hers) is an elementary teacher in Washington, DC. She recently received a master's degree in urban education and a graduate certificate in antiracism in education from the University of North Carolina at Charlotte. As a teacher she dedicates herself to learning from those who have led the way in antiracist work and to empowering young students to have agency over their own lives.

Scott R. Gartlan (he/him/his) is executive director of the Charlotte Teachers Institute. He is a former high school teacher and counselor. He has supported the growth and development of more than five hundred PK–12h grade teachers through high-quality professional development seminars and programs. His work focuses on effective teacher professional development, teacher efficacy, and program evaluation.

Oluseun "Seun" Omitoogun (she/her/hers) is the DEI Manager for College Forward. Her personal, professional, and academic passions are driven by the study of positive racial identity development in curriculum and antiracist pedagogy. This passion inspired her as lead innovator of an antiracist curriculum at Central Park School for Children (CPSC), where she also worked as a seventh-grade English language arts teacher. Her work led her to serve as CPSC's inaugural Equity Coach, a position that she helped develop and still serves as a consultant for.

Elizabeth Veilleux Haynes (she/her/hers) is serving as an Auxiliar de Conversación in a public school in Murcia, Spain, for the coming year. For the last five years, Elizabeth served as a social studies teacher at South Mecklenburg High School in Charlotte Mecklenburg Schools teaching courses such as American History II, the Big History Project, AP Psychology, and AVID 12. Elizabeth will begin her masters at the University of Washington in education policy and leadership in 2023.

www.ingramcontent.com/pod-product-compliance
Lightning Source LLC
Chambersburg PA
CBHW021900230426
43671CB00006B/461